THE

INDIGO

PRESS

THESE BONES WILL RISE AGAIN

THE

INDIGO

PRESS

THE MOOD INDIGO
ESSAY SERIES

THESE BONES WILL RISE AGAIN

PANASHE CHIGUMADZI

THE

INDIGO

PRESS

MOOD INDIGO

An imprint of The Indigo Press

50 Albemarle Street

London W1S 4BD

www.theindigopress.com

The Indigo Press Limited Reg. No. 10995574

Registered Office: Wellesley House, Duke of Wellington Avenue

Royal Arsenal, London SE18 6SS

ISBN 978-1-9996833-0-6

eBook ISBN 978-1-9996833-1-3

Design by www.salu.io

Typeset in Goudy Old Style by www.beyondwhitespace.com

Printed and bound in Great Britain

by TJ International, Padstow

MIX

Paper from
responsible sources

FSC® C013056

Kuna Mbuya Lilian Chigumadzi née Dzumbira

Ndima yenyu makapedza

History is created
in the mouth

Yvonne Vera

History is messy for the
people who must live it

Michel-Rolph Trouillot
Silencing the Past: Power and the Production of History

I

'Mudzimu waivepiko, mudzimu mukuru isu tichi-
netseka?'

The Jairos Jiri Band asks this of me as I listen to them
over my iPhone speaker. Where was our ancestor spirit,
our great ancestor, while we were suffering? Someone
had just sent their song 'Take Cover' to one of the
many WhatsApp groups keeping me updated with the
latest in fake and genuine news of what was happening
in Zimbabwe. The day before we had seen the videos of
tanks moving on the outskirts of Harare after army chief
Constantino Chiwenga denounced Robert Mugabe's
sacking of then Vice-President Emmerson Mnangagwa.
My friends in Zimbabwe told me about the gunfire they
heard. By the morning we had all seen the shaky recordings
of the Zimbabwe Broadcasting Corporation (ZBC)

announcement in which Major General Sibusiso Busi Moyo declared that the army had taken over. Apparently it was not a coup. Mugabe was safe. They were 'only targeting criminals around him'. The army was merely safeguarding the revolution, lest it be betrayed.

When I forward the clip of 'Take Cover' to my friend, she in turn shares her recordings of the Chimurenga music playing on ZBC that morning. She says she is feeling patriotic. Apparently, so are a number of other Zimbabweans on my Twitter timeline.

Zimbabwe has had many versions of history. The history of this moment, that some are already beginning to tell, is that this is the 'Fourth Chimurenga'.

As I listen to the Jairos Jiri Band, I am unsteady. Mugabe's impending removal feels as if the bottom half of one of Zimbabwe's famous granite balancing rocks is being dislodged while we are still sitting on top of it. Where we are, suspended perilously above the ground, is not good, but where are we going to fall? What are we going to fall onto?

There are many questions and I am looking for answers. The kind of answers that slip past the facts of history books or analyses by pundits and experts. Answers that are not party politics. That are not Zimbabwe African National Union – Patriotic Front (ZANU–PF), or Zimbabwe African People's Union (ZAPU) or the Movement for Democratic Change (MDC). Answers that are not Cecil John Rhodes, Ian Smith, Joshua Nkomo, Robert Mugabe, Morgan Tsvangirai or Emmerson Mnangagwa, or any other Big Men in the history of the nation. Instead, the answers I need are answers to politics that are about how we live, hope, dream, cry, laugh, pray and believe. As I search, I realize that if I want different answers, I need different questions. The kind that the Jairos Jiri Band is asking: 'Where was our ancestor spirit, our great ancestor, while we were suffering?'

In the midst of the confusion, I turn to a more familiar song: Thomas Mapfumo's 'Mhondoro'. My Shona is proficient but not literary. The long-exiled Mapfumo, whose lyrics are less ambiguous in their revolutionary message, should have been far easier for me to understand. He had not really featured in our household, despite the fact that he, along with family favourite, Oliver Mtukudzi, played music based on the mbira dzevadzimu, the mbira of the ancestors, an instrument of the Shona people, discouraged from being played by both missionaries and the Rhodesian state. The colonizers were right. They recognized that the mbira is dangerous – a mouth through which spirits can stir up their people.

I had 'discovered' Mapfumo on my own in the last few years. His *Greatest Hits* album is in my car, so I look for him on YouTube. In the video I often play, we hear Mapfumo's deep bass explaining the song before it starts. This song, like many songs of the mbira, is one that is used for communication between the living and the dead. When it is sung, the ancestors, communicating through the spirit mediums, tell the living what they should know about the past, present and future.

As a people who believe that a person is both flesh and spirit and lives on after death, we often commune with our ancestors, but it is especially in times of crisis and need that we look to them for answers about ourselves. Answers that fall outside the categories of birth and death, that move with and against time, that collapse time, that are of and outside a place, that perhaps only a mudzimu, a familial ancestor spirit, or a mhondoro, a royal ancestor spirit, can provide.

Singing as if he is witnessing a spirit medium being possessed by an ancestor, Mapfumo declares that Zimbabwe is the land of the mhondoro. Those who fought in the Chimurenga looked to the royal ancestral spirits to guide and lead them. This is how the war was won. In his words, I can feel I am closer to the heart of what defines our people, a deeper truth that eludes news reports and punditry.

In my search for the questions to ask in order to understand these events, there is one statement that keeps coming back to me: 'Mapfupa angu achapfuka.' *My bones will rise again.*

27 April 1898. It is the answer that the spirit medium of the ancestor Mbuya Nehanda, who had lived in the Mazowe Valley of north-east Zimbabwe, gave when she faced the question posed by the noose in vicious response to her spiritual and military leadership of the Ndebele-Shona uprisings of 1896–97 against Cecil John Rhodes'

Pioneer Column. The First 'Chimurenga' as it is known in chiShona. 'Umvukela' in isiNdebele. She knew that the noose did not question her alone; it questioned and mocked us all. 'Look, your great spirit mediums are just flesh and blood. Where is the spirit now?' Her answer, before the noose took her breath, was simple. My bones will rise again. The fire of these words was shut up in the bones that were buried in an unmarked grave. Bones that go into the earth and rise again and again. For decades, the embers of her bones would burn in resistance.

28 April 1966. A farm in Chinhoyi, northern Zimbabwe. Almost seventy years and a day since Mbuya Nehanda was buried in an unmarked grave. The fire of her bones was finally released in the barrel of the guns held by the Chinhoyi Seven: David Guzuzu. Arthur Maramba. Christopher Chatambudza. Simon Chingozha Nyandoro. Godfrey Manyerenyere. Godwin Dube. Chubby Savanhu. Theirs was the first salvo fired against Ian Smith's Unilateral Declaration of Independence (UDI). It was the first strike by the military wing of ZANU against Rhodesia's stubborn clinging onto white minority-rule – even as the winds of change, inaugurating majority-ruled states, were blowing across the African continent. Smith's men, the Rhodesian Army, overwhelmed the Chinhoyi Seven on that farm. All seven dead. New bones for the earth.

13 August 1967. The next salvo would be released in Hwange Game Reserve in western Zimbabwe. ZAPU's military wing combined forces with fighters from South

Africa, the African National Congress's (ANC's) military wing, for their joint campaign against the settler minority regimes in South Africa and Rhodesia. Smith's men intercepted members of the eighty-man-strong campaign and the first of many battles began. Over the next month, clashes claimed even more lives. Bones for the earth.

The Chinhoyi and Hwange conflagrations would blaze into the Second Chimurenga of the 1970s. As that revolutionary fire spread throughout the country, the spirit medium of Mbuya Nehanda, then living in Dande Valley in north-western Zimbabwe, would guide the comrades.

Bones conjure up a numerical inversion of dates. Colonization in 1890. Independence in 1980. Zimbabwe arrives. Bones continue to rattle with fire, but few will hear them. These are the 1980s. We are busy shouting the praises of new roads, schools and hospitals. Swords are turning into ploughshares as we are flattering each other with reconciliatory rhetoric between Black and White. We will deal with land later. Guns are rattling in Matabeleland and the Midlands, thousands are dead for their 'dissidentry'. But elsewhere in the land we cannot hear them. We are renaming buildings and streets and aircraft after our ancestral spirits but we will not listen to the bones.

Then come the 1990s. We are weighed down by an economic downturn. Structural Adjustment Programmes. Organized labour and civil society protesting price increases and job losses. War veterans demanding compensation, including pensions and land. We go profit and adventure seeking in the Democratic Republic of Congo's war. These are the 2000s. We are now taking over the land that was promised to us. This is the Third Chimurenga. Hyper-inflation and economic free fall. 2008. Violence and vote rigging. A government of national unity is patched together. Some economic reprieve. 2013. We are back to the same. The years go by as we fight just to survive. We can barely hear ourselves through the noise of our daily struggles.

What has happened to us?
It has been a few years since I came to realize that neither the questions nor the answers I need will come from the places I usually search. Party-political answers cannot tell you enough about my people and what has brought us to this place. In search of those answers, I must lower my eyes from the heights of Big Men who have created a history that does not know little people, let alone little women, except as cannon fodder.

For a long time I have wanted to listen to my paternal grandmother, Mbuya Lilian Chigumadzi, talk about her life. I have lived in South Africa since I was three, so time, distance and language have been barriers. I took time for granted. All of a sudden it was taken away from me. The earth pulled me down as my grandmother's bones were taken into the ground. She is buried on 8 October 2017. I cannot be there to witness it but I feel the weight of her interred bones from thousands of kilometres away. The dislocation I have felt all these years comes in its full force to destabilize me. The only way I can bear the weight is to remember bones that go into the earth and rise again and again. I have to remember that my family and I may have lost her physical presence, but we have also gained an ancestor spirit, a mudzimu.

15 November 2017. Just over a month later, my sense of dislocation is heightened as we are suddenly being liberated from Mugabe's rule by the very military that supported him for almost four decades. I cannot believe that it is happening. Believe it, some say. This is the Fourth Chimurenga. All fourteen days of it. Politics comes at you fast.

In this moment of great upheaval, who has time to listen? I have to still the world around me. There is much confusion and much noise, so I struggle to hear the bones of Mbuya Nehanda and Mbuya Chigumadzi rattling in my heart. I have to still myself, make myself steady, so I can listen, so I can hear what these spirits have to say.

II

At the foot of a hill behind the musha, the homestead, belonging to my great-grandfather, Sekuru Ifayi Dzumbira, there is San rock art painted on granite outcrops, etched in vivid reds and brown. Hundreds, if not thousands, of years old, the images painted here are older than Zimbabwe.

It is 26 December 2017. We have driven almost 70 km from my maternal grandmother Mbuya Beneta Chiganze's home in Gandiya village of Makoni District. Our visit is to my late paternal grandmother Mbuya Lilian Chigumadzi's surviving relatives living in Mutare, Zimbabwe's fourth-largest city, located in the eastern highlands, on the border with Mozambique.

We begin 20 km outside of Mutare in Dora Dombo, a ruzheva, or what used to be called a 'native reserve'.

This was where my father had always known his maternal grandfather Sekuru Ifayi Dzumbira to live and so he had assumed this to have been 'kumusha kwaMbuya Chigumadzi', her ancestral home. The homestead is tucked into a valley surrounded by towering granite mountains. As we approach Sekuru's home, my father points to the adjacent mountain: 'It used to be said that there was a njuzu that lived on top of it.' As the surviving children of my great-grandfather's second wife show us to Sekuru Ifayi's grave at the foot of a set of hills, they confirm that the menacing water spirit is still there. They know, because whenever rain is about to fall, it is always preceded by the sight of smoke at the top of the mountain where there is a stream. They take us to the cave-like rock overhang, just behind the homestead, under which Sekuru Ifayi practised his profession as an iron smelter. We pose for pictures with the remnants of his tools and implements.

Together, the imposing granite rocks on which the age-old art stood and under which my great-grandfather carried out his traditional blacksmithery would have made the perfect foundation for an origin story. A rock-solid monument to the past on which to stake my family's claim to Zimbabwe and its history.

My own struggle for history begins in dislocation. Having grown up in South Africa, away from my extended family, I've always been at a physical remove from my culture. The kind of 'loss' of heritage that I experienced is maybe best understood through my relationship to my mother tongue. At some point, my brother and I had 'forgotten' Shona. I couldn't tell you how exactly it happened. It felt a swift and painless process: I arrived at my predominantly white pre-school in the South African coastal city of Durban not speaking a word of English and, within a short amount of time, I could barely speak any Shona, despite my parents speaking it at home.

By the time I was a pre-adolescent child, Zimbabwe was dipping into crisis. Since independence in 1980, the government had been under pressure to deracialize an economy firmly invested in the domestic white landowning class allied with international capital. By 2000, liberation war veterans were fed up with the government's refusal to shake up an agricultural sector dominated by 4,500 mostly white large-scale commercial farmers. Over that year's Easter weekend the war veterans staged a carefully organized campaign, seeing 170,000 families occupy 3,000 white-owned farms. Initially opposing the move, the increasingly unpopular ZANU–PF government backed the war veterans, sanctioning the chaos that Shona-speaking Zimbabweans refer to as jambanja that would characterize the Fast Track Land Reform Programme's initial stages. The jambanja spread to the economy too as inflation began to rise, the currency became worthless, and queues outside supermarkets, banks, fuel stations, hospitals and workplaces became longer and longer. Living in Polokwane, 220 km from Beitbridge, which soon became the busiest of all the continent's border posts, we felt the effects of this crisis keenly. Every other weekend relatives would stay over to stockpile groceries unavailable on the shelves back home and the town was inundated by poorer 'border jumpers' who were illegally crossing the wide Limpopo River into South Africa to god-knows-what fortune. I was now being called a 'kwerekwere', a pejorative for black foreigners, at school.

The stories we found in books and listened to from the mouths of my parents as we made frequent journeys back home held me as steady as they could against the onslaught of the dislocation. My maternal grandfather Sekuru Douglas Chiganze, or 'Teacher Chiganze', a primary school teacher, would often buy us Shona school readers. More than just basic literacy, this was a way for me to get to read and hear some of the stories and fables that my grandmothers would have told me had I grown up with them close by. Long before I had the consciousness to buy and eventually write my own stories, this was my first interaction with the literature of my country.

I have not been the only one to struggle for a hold on history. Having gone through the trauma of one of the continent's most bitter liberation wars, Zimbabwe is a country that has come to be defined by struggle: over independence, over land, over citizenship, over the 'authentic nation'. Central to all this is the struggle over history.

Over the centuries there have been many official versions. In the colonial imagination, history proper: that is, the history of Europeans in Africa, begins with the British colonial encounter in 1890. And because their violent occupation of land met with resistance by the Africans in the region, British settlers had to justify their right of conquest by creative means.

Within that realm, Wilbur Smith, that great chronicler of the White Man's Burden in Africa, was arguably at his finest in his 1972 novel, *The Sunbird*. In it, Smith narrates the allegory of Great Zimbabwe as his protagonists, South African archaeologists, 'discover' an abandoned ancient city named Opet, which they believe to have been founded by 'fair-skinned, golden-haired warriors from across the sea, who mined the gold, enslaved the indigenous tribes and flourished for hundreds of years'. Initially, the evidence points to founders of 'obscure Bantu origin', but eventually the truth is revealed that the founders were Phoenicians from Carthage. The fabulous Opet had once been the centre of a great civilization which included Zimbabwe and many other towns, which had met its downfall around 450 AD when it was destroyed by black invaders.

Disappointing in its unoriginality, Smith's narrative plot was just the sort of myth rife in the Rhodesian imagination. If the conquest of 'unoccupied' land along with the minerals beneath it and people on top of it was justified through the *terra nullius* principle, then the settlers also imagined the history of the land and people they conquered as a no-man's land.

Time and history were colonized so that they acquired

a new racial dimension: the natives they ruled over were backward, ahistorical, primitive tribesmen who were, in effect, out of time. The settlers mapped out an imaginary space in which Africans, made up of docile Shona people terrorized by the cruel damnable race of Ndebele, became part of the hostile natural environment that had to be conquered for the development of a civilized white man's country that would take on the name of Rhodesia. In this battle for time and history, the ancient civilization of Great Zimbabwe built out of the landscape's granite stones was a thorn in the side of the Rhodesian settlers, who defended their right of conquest on the grounds that the very same native tribesmen whose ancestors had built the city had only recently come down from out of the trees.

Published just as the African nationalists began to wage the liberation war, Wilbur Smith's allegory about the ruined state of Great Zimbabwe reinforced a sense of emergency. The urgency of self-defence was illustrated by the downfall of the great ancient white civilization that did not realize in time the danger of the Black Peril. The patriotic histories, underwritten by white arrogance and their perceived invincibility drove the Rhodesians to take up arms for 'their land', singing their hymn, 'Rhodesians Never Die'.

In the decades leading up to this war for the return of land, African nationalists had already begun the war for their own history. Great Zimbabwe was re-appropriated as a symbol of a proud African past and by the early 60s, following nationalist leader Michael Mawema's original use of the name, meaning 'the house of stone', to refer to the country, liberation movements were naming themselves for Zimbabwe.

In 1956, driven by a desire to show that Africans were not, to use Ayi Kwei Armah's words, 'a people of yesterday', ZANU founding president Ndabaningi Sithole published the first Ndebele novel, *Umvukela waMaNdebele* (The Ndebele Uprising), which depicted the 1893 and 1896 wars of resistance against the British. That same year, Solomon Mutswairo allegorized a pre-colonial golden age with the Shona novel *Feso*. In the book, a poem that would become a rallying cry for Africans battling against colonial rule, 'O Nehanda Nyakasikana' (Oh Nehanda Feminine Spirit), called on the guardian ancestral spirit of Mbuya Nehanda to come and rescue her people from slavery. The novel would be banned but by the Second Chimurenga the famous prayer to Mbuya Nehanda's spirit would come to be recited at pungwes, all-night political vigils, alongside the song, 'Mbuya Nehanda kufa vachitaura shuwa'. Mbuya Nehanda died speaking the truth.

By the turn of the century, as the post-independence government faced the fallout from fast-track land reform, Mbuya Nehanda continued to be central to the official version of the past which reduced a complex history of nationalism to three-part episodes of Chimurenga. In this telling, former President Robert Mugabe was the spiritual heir of the revered mediums of the ancestors Mbuya Nehanda and Sekuru Kaguvi who led the First

Chimurenga against the British colonizers from 1896–97. Along with ZANU, the liberation party founded in 1963, Mugabe led the Second Chimurenga, an armed guerrilla conflict against the unilaterally declared 'independent' Rhodesian white minority-rule government of Ian Smith. Independence and majority rule were finally declared in 1980. Mugabe and his party continued in that same revolutionary spirit in what would be named the Third Chimurenga – the radical land redistribution of the 2000s. In a twist of fate, it is this very Chimurenga legacy that the war veterans and military were claiming to defend against 'enemies' and 'criminal elements' when they intervened in ZANU–PF party politics in November 2017 to force Mugabe's ouster.

This official version of what Terence Ranger named 'patriotic history' itself draws on a tradition in which the contributions of workers', women's, urban and other movements in the 'inter-Chimurenga' years are often erased or dismissed as merely reformist precursors to the nationalist era of the 50s and 60s. In both tellings, a straightforward story of suppression and revival reduces Chimurenga to a gun and, often, to a phallocentric struggle, ignoring the complex ways in which Africans did more than act out a false consciousness, but subverted and negotiated with the colonial state, continuously drawing on Chimurenga's intergenerational spirit to make and remake themselves after the military and spiritual conquest of the 1890s.

The struggles over history are complex, because the present continuously slips into the past, marking history as always ambivalent, incomplete, a work in progress. When we pick apart linear histories of cause and effect, we are bound to discover that history doesn't march forward in a straight line of progress. Instead, history is like water – it lives between us, and comes to us in waves. At times, it is still and unobtrusive, and, at others, it is turbulent and threatening. Even at its most innocuous, water poses hidden dangers, enclosing contested histories, and so we are always living in the tension between water's tranquillity and its tumult. When we walk along the water's edge, it's easy to take for granted the complex process of how that water reached our feet, to overlook what is washed away, what alters and what holds in the sands of time. It is an openness to history as a series of waves, always moving, always in a state of flux, always a site of discovery in the past, present and future, and not as something stable, foreclosed, frozen in the past, that is most troubling to nationalist agendas, because it is too difficult to control.

In the midst of these moving waves, quite far from the sturdy surface of Sekuru Dzumbira's granite boulders, the history that I am trying to craft begins with a moment etched on a surface that is man-made and far more flimsy. Perhaps less because of the surface's fragility and more because of the dislocations and disjunctures across generations and space, this is a history that begins with loss.

The unsteady surface is, or rather, was, a studio photograph of Mbuya Lilian Chigumadzi as a young woman. I don't know whether it still exists. As a schoolchild, this photograph was entrusted to my possession. I subsequently lost it, having, ironically, used it for a school project on family history. In it, she stands graceful, composed, sexy even. Her weight is on her left leg and her right hip is slightly tilted. A white cotton dress, stark against her dark skin, stretches a little over a rounded tummy and slim hips. A conical head wrap, the kind worn by Miriam Makeba, crowns her head. Lips parted, revealing a cheeky gap to swallow the world. She doesn't smile; there's nothing gratuitous here. Eyes wide, she meets my gaze, demanding that I bear witness.

Her statement, if I hear her correctly: un-bought and un-baased. Just arrived in Umtali, with no young man preparing to persuade any uncles for cattle he has not yet worked to own; no white family with dirty kitchens which need cleaning and children who need raising. Alone, unburdened, unattached, only Belonging to Herself.

Or so it is, in my imagining.

I look again. I sometimes see, in this black-and-white photo, something else. The photograph appeared to have been taken in the 1960s; she would have been around my age, her early twenties. A black-and-white photo with contrasts softened by years of the sun, her future receding into the monotony of her work, only for little sparks to be dulled by the weight of everyone else's future but her own.

I sometimes see in her statement, the one to which she demands I bear witness, an epitaph that life has taught me: sometimes, dreams are colder than death.

I have always felt profoundly sad about my childish negligence, because, to my knowledge, this was the only individual portrait taken of my grandmother for at least a few decades. Perhaps this is what I loved the most about that picture: that she was alone. That in that moment, she stood with no baby in her arms or on her back or husband by her side. I remember looking at the photo and always being struck by the ways in which she didn't look like the grandmother I knew. And perhaps this is the point; she is not my grandmother in that picture. She is not Mbuya Chigumadzi, Mai Chigumadzi, Mrs Kenneth Chigumadzi, Mai Rophina, Tete Lilian, Yaya Lily. She just is. She belongs to no one but herself. She is Lilian. That is who I find myself mourning, more than I mourn my grandmother.

On the day Mbuya died, I felt the earth pull me down. I couldn't sleep, I couldn't read, I couldn't watch TV. I think I could accept the death of Mbuya, because I had known that person. What I found difficult to accept was the death of the Lilian Dzumbira that I did not know. That is the person for whom I felt the deepest sense of loss. Unsure of what to do, I attempted to write down some questions.

What were you like as a child? What was your mother like? What about your grandmother?

Mbuya Lilian met Sekuru Kenneth Chigumadzi when he was working as a clerk near Mutare.

How did you meet Sekuru? Was it hard to live apart when he worked away in town? What did it mean to become a young widow with five children?

She had a stroke that paralyzed her twenty-three years ago.

Do you remember the experience of your stroke? Do you think it was your body forcing you to rest after all those years of hard work? What kept you going all these years?

I don't have much recollection of her walking, except for the time she and Mbuya Chiganze came to visit us in Durban a few months before her stroke.

What was it like to take a bus and leave the country for the first time? What about seeing the sea?

About Zimbabwe.

You used to ask when we would come back to Zimbabwe. What made you stop asking?

To my mind, my life, freed by the almost limitless opportunities of my time, and her life, limited by the circumstances of her day, seemed to exist on planes so far apart. For years, I looked at her, and other black women, with the eyes of the world clouded by a disturbing shallowness that does not allow for realities too far from my own experiences and my own time. It wasn't until I met the force of the unflinching stories of our mothers and grandmothers and aunts and sisters written by black women writers – Yvonne Vera, Ama Ata Aidoo, Alice Walker, Toni Morrison, Audre Lorde, Maryse Condé – that I was compelled to sit down and ask more of my view of their worlds, forcing me to find an answer to the question: what did it mean for a black woman to *be* in my grandmother's time?

Where I find myself in my writing, Mbuya found fulfilment in embodying a saying she often repeated: 'Mukadzi haagariri mawoko'. A woman does not sit idly on her hands. With those hands, she built a rich world as a caregiver, farmer, gardener, cook, baker, needleworker, doily-maker – cultivating a spirituality that is the very basis of the worlds about which I attempt to write.

When we visited my grandmother she often had the radio on, listening intently to the news, the talk shows and music of the day. Sometimes when I'd leave she would tease me saying, 'Panashe, we will talk on Facebook.' When we lamented the changing weather patterns, she would comment, 'I think it's this issue of global warming making this happen.' Her little cell phone was always ringing, the young and old alike calling to ask her for advice on this or that life matter. If it wasn't on the phone, they came to consult her directly in the bedroom that my family called the 'head office' or 'the court'. That is how she survived twenty-two years after a stroke. That is not the work of the body. That is the work of the spirit.

III

I meet her gaze again.

Mbuya steps into the studio. A cameraman is directing her to pose like glamorous women who appear in publications such as *African Parade*, *Bantu Mirror* and the *African Weekly*. Who took this photo? A John Mauluka, or Bester Kanyama of Southern Rhodesia's studios? Which were the studios that this young African woman could have stepped into? Salisbury's Amato Studios? Highfield's Rhodesian Studios? Rusape's Makoni Studios? Bulawayo's S. Pontonjie Photographic Studios? Whichever studio she found herself in, she was a young African marking her moment in history, at a time heavy with transformation, disjuncture and dislocation.

I set about reconstructing her image.

'**M**buya?'

'Woye?'

My maternal grandmother Mbuya Beneta Chiganze's soft reedy voice reassures me about the tentative start I am making. I continue in Shona.

'Mbuya, there are things I would like to ask you about your life tomorrow evening. Please be prepared.'

'About my life?'

'Ehe.'

'What exactly do you want to know?'

'Things like where you came from, where you were born, what was your mother's name. Things like that.'

'What are you going to do with it?'

'I would just like to know nhoroondo ye mhuri. This morning before we left kwaMurehwa I sat with vanatete and they told me a lot about our family and where we came from.'

'Are you writing a book?'

I do not want to say yes because my idea is still to focus the book I am writing on Mbuya Chigumadzi.

It is Christmas Eve. It takes time to convince Mbuya Chiganze. I explain that I had done something similar that very morning before we had left kwaMurehwa. My father's youngest sister Tete Evie, my grandfather's three surviving sisters, Tetes Ena, Evert and Venencia and I sat together to draw a family tree five generations back to 'Tateguru' Chigumadzi, the first to come to what would become Murehwa communal lands.

Driving from Murehwa to Gandiya village, around 85 km west of Mutare, my family and I had already gotten the sense that this Christmas, the first 'post-Mugabe', felt a little different. The Harare–Mutare highway which used to be riddled with potholes had been regraded in the last two years and, thanks to the military coup-not-a-coup which had reined in the powers of the Zimbabwe Republic Police, there were no road blocks to harass and extract bribes every 50 km. It should have been a less stressful drive, except the roads were full of motorists cutting corners and overtaking on blind curves, impatient to spend Christmas kumusha. We were delayed by the seemingly kilometres-long queues at the Rusape tollgate, an innovation of the more economically savvy 2009–13 Government of National Unity between ZANU-PF and the MDC. On a two-lane highway, drivers take the initiative to create six lanes. There are queues for EcoCash mobile money payments, and queues for cash payments. And, as if to spite us – the citizenry – for having had their hands tied by the 'new dispensation' in the aftermath of the coup-not-a-coup, the few police officials on duty don't do much more than occasionally point a half-hearted finger here and there before returning to their phones or folding their arms. Having survived the tollgate, our grocery stop in Rusape's OK supermarket had also taken longer than usual. Unlike other years, there are queues of people eager to eat Christmas well. These delays mean that, despite our mid-morning departure from Murehwa, we fail to arrive in

Gandiya village before nightfall as is usual, much to Mbuya Chiganze's dismay.

As soon as the familiar sign in front of Mbuya Chiganze's gate, 'NDAPOTA VHARAI GEDHI!', PLEASE CLOSE THE GATE!, appeared, I had already begun trying to persuade myself to ask her about her personal history. The tall matriarch stood waiting to welcome us with my mother's only sister, Mainini Foro. I continued to bargain with myself until we retired to bed. Although there are several spare bedrooms, with long stretches between visits I prefer the intimacy of sleeping with Mbuya and Mainini. Mbuya refused, as usual, to sleep on her bed. She laid out her mattress, while Mainini and I took the bed.

That evening there is much activity on the dust road. Kombis are going up and down with relatives coming from town. Lying in the dark, we are listening out for the sound of my uncle, Sekuru Timothy, the oldest of this house, arriving from Harare. We think it is one of them passing Mbuya's gate but it isn't. The radio is too loud, blasting one of 2017's hits, Jah Prayzah's 'Ndini ndamubata'. I'm the one who caught her. Mainini and Mbuya agree that this has been one of the busiest Christmases in a while. The 'new dispensation' seems to have generated confidence. People seem to be spending money and making the journey home to celebrate and enact the hope of good times ahead.

As we listen to the night's activities, I'm still bargaining with myself. Eventually, the sting of my regret over not having spoken to Mbuya Chigumadzi finally pushes me to make a tentative start. Suspicious though she is, Mbuya Chiganze eventually agrees. She makes me promise that I will have whatever I write translated into Shona so that she will be able to read it. I know she will. Every available surface of her bedroom is topped with biblical literature, Shona school readers, self- and agricultural improvement guides and many copies of the Shona language daily, *Kwayedza*, notorious for its splash stories of witchcraft and scandal.

Sometimes we stumble over language. Mainini is a bridge between Mbuya's deep Manyika dialect and my Manyika-Zezuru hodgepodge. Mbuya repeats the phrase, 'Bhabha wedhu wekudhenga.' 'Our Father in heaven.' She is imitating the accented Shona of the white Anglican priests. She says this is what I sometimes sound like. Sometimes she gets frustrated with my line of questioning. 'Zvimwe hazvibvunzwi.' Some things are just not asked about. 'How could I have asked my own mother such a thing?' Sometimes I am not sure how to continue asking as she relays difficult experiences. It feels cruel, voyeuristic, to ask her to tell me more about what it was like for her and her family to be put into the lorries that carried them from their original musha to a place they did not know during the forced removals of her girlhood, or to ask her to describe how she felt when she saw the school trunk returning home on top of the bus without its owner, her third-born son, just fourteen years old, confirming that he had not started his second year at St Faith's as they had expected, but had hitch-hiked to Mozambique with friends to join the Chimurenga. 'To cry? You could not. You just had to keep it to yourself. This was war.'

On Christmas morning, I am surprised, and relieved, that we only wake after five, prompted by my going to the toilet. My eighty-four-year-old grandmother is notorious for waking up at 4 a.m., soon after the first cockcrow. You will be woken up by the sound of her loud talk with Mainini and her beginning to go about her business, getting ready to go into her field by the time the sun rises. In the past, Mama says, they were often woken at this time by the sound of Teacher and Mbuya Chiganze praying and singing hymns.

The morning, after sweeping Mbuya's yard, cleaning the house and sitting down to breakfast, is spent visiting Teacher Chiganze's surviving siblings and their families. When we return, Sekuru Timothy and his wife have finally arrived. Joined by two other relatives from the village, we sit on Mbuya's veranda for Christmas lunch. Mainini has cooked. From Mbuya's grinding mill, we have sadza rezviyo, stiff millet porridge; from her garden, green vegetables and okra and, from the butcher, chicken for stew. We eat leisurely, in time following up the heavy meal with a dessert of freshly cooked mealie cobs. I have my notebooks and recorder out that afternoon as I begin to ask them about their experiences of the liberation war. That night, we sit with Mbuya and stay up late reconstructing a family tree going back four generations.

On the morning we leave, Mbuya hands me an album containing old photographs; I have been asking for them for years, to no avail. Here is Mbuya Chiganze as a young unmarried woman; Mbuya and Teacher Chiganze on their wedding day in 1955; Teacher Chiganze and his cousin as young men and Mama as a toddler on Mbuya's lap. There are more than fifty images I've never seen. For the sake of my family, I contain my tears.

I am trusted once again with these photos. I scan the many fading pictures, preserving them in digital memory. No future grandchild will lose them in their excitement to show their friends or teachers at school. In the weeks that follow, I gaze and gaze at the photos. They are providing new textures to the histories that have been narrated to me.

As I scan the pictures meticulously, I take care to study the studio stamps and hand-written inscriptions on the back of the photos. At the back of a studio photo of Mbuya Chiganze's late brother, I make out a fading purple stamp: 'Panakromatic Studios. Sakubva PO BOX. Lovemore M—a'.

'Sekuru Justine, do you know the photographer who was named Lovemore?'

'Ehe! Lovemore Mtema.'

'Yes! Do you know where his studio was? You will show us when we go to Sakubva, hanti Sekuru?'

Sekuru Justine Dzumbira laughs. This muzaya of his is troublesome. It is 12 January 2018. I am trying to persuade my great-uncle Justine, Mbuya Chigumadzi's youngest and only surviving brother (from the same mother), to show us around the township of Sakubva. This, and not Dora Dombo, I have 'discovered' is where the family had lived as children. I have returned to Zimbabwe to see Sekuru Justine in the New Year. He lives on a mountain slope just south of Mutare. If you want to be accurate, 'pa16-maira', a reference to the old mile distance markers on the Mutare–Chimanimani highway.

Mainini Foro and my cousin, and her small baby, had left Harare for Mutare at 7 a.m. By eleven o'clock, Mainini's car was parked at the house of one of Mbuya's widowed sisters-in-law at the bottom of the mountain. With a screaming baby on my back, groceries in hand, my aunt and cousin following behind, I crossed the road and walked half a kilometre past a stream and up rocky paths that cars cannot pass through.

For our efforts, Mbuya Jane Dzumbira has fried for us. Road-runners, guinea fowl eggs, potatoes, yellow rice, pumpkin. We are all full, but have second helpings. Mbuya beams. When we had visited on Boxing Day last year, the fried goat meat she had brought out had been the initial consolation to my disappointment that her husband Sekuru Justine, who was to tell me all I wanted to know about his sister Mbuya Lilian, had long gone to town.

The consummate host, Mbuya Jane could barely sit down as she rushed to serve us the fried goat meat, a compromise after we had politely declined her cooking a full meal. While we ate, she retold the story of my father and her brother-in-law building her a mud and pole 'kitchen' in 1979. She could hardly contain herself, recounting that the 'kitchen situation' in the ruzevha was such a culture shock for her that her siblings had come to take her to look for work in Harare, because her family had left the rural areas many generations ago. I took less note of the salty sweet goat in my hand and began to listen more carefully, so that later, as she held my hand while escorting us down the mountain, I could ask more.

'Mbuya, are you saying you were a born-rukesheni?'

'Ehe!'

This was my girl. In the last few days I had discovered that Mbuya Chigumadzi also had this unusual experience of being a 'born-rukesheni', which implied many things about time, space and identity. White settlers lived in towns and farms, while black people were corralled into the ruzheva, and later the rukesheni, 'native locations' or 'African townships' in the urban areas. The rukesheni, a place representing chimanjemanje, things of the now, was never supposed to be anyone's home, only the dormitory you slept in while working in the white man's town. When your work with the white man was finished, you would always return kumusha, a place embodying chinyakare, things of the past. It was only those who were 'rootless' and 'uncultured' and didn't have any musha to return to, like the many migrant labourers from Zambia, Malawi, Mozambique and South Africa, who would make a permanent home of the townships and bear born-rukesheni children like Mbuya Lilian and Mbuya Jane.

Further along the mountain, Mbuya Jane explained how her family came to be 'rootless' three generations back: her grandmother had worked as a nanny in the town of Umtali, now Mutare. She was one of the few African women who lived in the colony's towns. Only a small minority of African women in these cities were formally employed as Mbuya Jane's grandmother was. This is how, generations later, Mbuya Jane came to meet Sekuru Justine, who, as she did not neglect to say, was a handsome young man living with his family at 264 Chineta Road in Sakubva, one of several of Umtali's townships.

After some hesitance, Sekuru Justine is persuaded by his muzaya. He is going to show us the studios and 264 Chineta Road. Using his wooden cane, he easily leads us down the mountain which is now home to several generations of Dzumbiras. Along the way, I try to find out more about earlier generations of the family but Sekuru does not know much about those before his grandparents because they died when he was a child.

I try to find the answer a different way. It can be said that if you want truly to understand a person and where they come from, you need to know their mutupo. A person's totem ties them to their original home and their people through a founding ancestor. These are ties inextricably linked to chinyakare, finding origin in times long past.

These ties pre-suppose any 'Zimbabwean-ness', and yet have come to define it. Those who are bound only to the city do not have it. They are, to use Mugabe's description of Zimbabweans of foreign descent, 'totemless'. Many of these totemless urban residents were among those most affected by ZANU–PF's Operation Murambatsvina. Taking place shortly after 2005's disputed parliamentary election, the campaign to 'get rid of the filth' in urban slum areas appeared to many to be retribution for voting the 'wrong' way.

I ask Sekuru what their mutupo is.

'Beta Wabata Dhliwayo.'

At first I think I'm not hearing him correctly. As a rule, we do not have 'l' in most Shona dialects. I want to tell Sekuru that this is not Shona he is speaking but I have to remind myself that even talking of Shona and 'Shona people', who today make up more than three-quarters of the population, is a misnomer. 'Shona-ness' is, in fact, a relatively recent and an external imposition from the complex interaction with white settlers, Ndebele, who now make up the largest minority at just less than a fifth of the population, and other peoples such as the Shangani, Venda and Tonga.

Seeing my confusion, he clarifies, 'Dhliwayo. Dhliwayo, like Lobengula. We came with Zwangendaba. We are maNdau.'

I nod. Sekuru's 'l' is of those Nguni clans who, in a period of great upheaval in Southern Africa, migrated from what is now the Kwa-Zulu Natal province in South Africa into the Zimbabwean plateau in the early- to mid-eighteenth century, often intermarrying and incorporating 'Shona' and other existing clans such as the Ndau into their new kingdoms. The Dhliwayo clan, who claim one Puzwayo as a founding ancestor, likely came here under the leadership of Zwangendaba Jele as had done the Khumalos, led by Mzilikazi, father of King Lobengula, and the founder of the Ndebele kingdom. Originally establishing themselves in the Chimanimani mountains, about 140 km from Mutare, the Dhliwayos were reputed military tacticians who were rewarded with land in the Penhalonga Valley, near the present site of Mutare, for assisting Mutasa's Manyika kingdom battle Makoni's Maungwe in the epic war, Hondo Huru yepaMhanda.

By the mid-1880s, the Dhliwayos found new adversaries as the discovery of gold brought British and Portuguese prospectors into the Penhalonga Valley. In July 1890, Cecil John Rhodes' British South Africa Company (BSAC) hoisted up the Union Jack in Salisbury and in November set up Mutare's first permanent white settlement after Mutasa had granted them a mining concession.

The history of Chimurenga has been related as if the first major anti-colonial resistance took place in 1896 and was the sole effort of the Shona people, but there is more to it than that. Many Africans saw this British invasion as yet another episode in their long history of anti-colonial resistance beginning with the Maputukezi, the Portuguese, in the sixteenth century. According to several historians, what should really be considered the First Chimurenga took place in the late-seventeenth century as Africans fought off would-be Portuguese colonialists. In these wars, 'Chimurenga', meaning 'Murenga's thing' or 'Murenga's war', became a Shona idiom of resistance in honour of the warrior ancestor Murenga Sororenzou.

In this spirit, the Ndebele resisted colonization in the 1893 war during which King Lobengula mysteriously disappeared. In 1896, secretly led by Lobengula's senior wife Lozikeyi Dlodlo, who had become Queen Regent, the Ndebele began their revolt in March with the guidance of priests of their ancestral religion. From June, Shona leaders such as Mashayamombe, working with Sekuru Kaguvi and Hwata, alongside Mbuya Nehanda, began their revolt. Together these would become what the Ndebele call the Umvukela, and the Shona, the First Chimurenga. A negotiated settlement ended the Matabeleland resistance as 1896 drew to a close, while the Mashonaland uprisings were brutally suppressed in early 1897. Military and spiritual conquests were symbolically cemented as the heads of several Chimurenga leaders including Makoni and Kunzvi Nyandoro, and the mediums of Mbuya Nehanda and Sekuru Kaguvi, were presented as trophies to Queen Victoria.

The end of the Chimurenga did not mean the end of colonial aggression. Violent land seizures followed, allocating significant lots of the best land to white miners and farmers so that Africans such as the Dzumbiras who, as Sekuru Justine explains, were hunters who moved from area to area in search of game, lost their livelihoods.

Around the time of Sekuru Ifayi Dzumbira's estimated birth in the 1920s, white settlers consolidated their power, voting in favour of a self-governing colony and against joining the Union of South Africa in a 1922 referendum. Naturally, self-governance excluded the natives, who, since their military defeat, had been forging new political traditions. They petitioned the mother country of Britain, as Nyamanda, King Lobengula's son, had done and, in a competing strategy, attempted to carve out space for political participation within the new colonial order as the Rhodesia Bantu Voters Association had done.

When his first child Lilian was born in 1940, Sekuru Ifayi Dzumbira and his wife Mbuya Perekedzai were living in the capital of the Gombakomba reserve, just outside Umtali. They were soon forcibly removed from the reserve by the settler government which feared the concentration of Africans in the area. The Dzumbiras joined many other displaced Africans in living on the compound of a nearby farm where, among other things, Sekuru Ifayi did carpentry work.

By the time their third child Misheck was born in 1945, Ifayi Dzumbira had found employment as a mechanic at Carlisle Enterprises in Umtali. With the end of the Second World War and the election of the National

Party in South Africa, Southern Rhodesia's white settlers enjoyed a new period of prosperity, while the economic position of Africans was seriously undermined by being deprived of land, the primary means of production in an economy based on agriculture and mineral extraction. The colony's industrializing economy increasingly depended on urbanized black workers, who soon began staging industrial action such as the 1945 Railway Workers' Strike and the 1948 General Strike. In the rural areas, there were further land pressures as the settler government awarded land to white war veterans, while it was not unheard of for the Africans who had fought alongside them to receive bicycles as compensation. Caught up in this upheaval, the Dzumbiras were forced to find accommodation in Sakubva, making the eldest child Mbuya Lilian not quite a 'born-rukesheni' in the strictest sense, but nonetheless a black Rhodesian woman with the unusual experience of growing up in the township.

IV

Driving north from the Chimanimani–Mutare highway, Mainini Foro turns her car left into Sakubva and onto Chineta Road. Sekuru Justine directs us to number 264. We drive slowly, carefully manoeuvring past the many people walking and standing around in the heavily potholed street. We pass the large outdoor flea market and turn right into a street full of makeshift tuck-shops, mechanics, hair salons and butchers in their front yards. In the time of Sekuru Justine's upbringing, Southern Rhodesia's townships were similarly designed with grids of identical cement-brick houses built along tidy streets. Over time, migrants deserting the ruzevha in search of work inundated these dormitory townships and conditions deteriorated and, in line with the extractive model of the colony, the tight-pursed authorities refused to allocate sufficient resources. As we approach Unit 264, it gets less busy. These are 'maNHB', National Housing Board houses, for married workers and their families. The homes in the street are identical: standalone four-room homes with small front yards. The other sections, such as the 'MacGregor's', where each man was quite literally allocated a door, and hostels where four to six men were allocated to a room, were for single workers. With the end of urban influx controls after Independence, the tide of people driven from the rural areas by economic pressure has not stemmed and so they now house entire families.

We head for Panokromatic Studios. I am convinced this is where my grandmother's photo was taken. My father had confirmed that the photo was taken around the time his parents had been courting. This was the only studio around then. From a water-damaged family photo of a beaming Sekuru Justine, youthful Mbuya Jane and their firstborn, taken at the Panokromatic Studios, I recognize the black-and-white flooring as the one that I had seen in Mbuya Lilian's photo.

'Did Lovemore Mtema take your photo?' I ask Sekuru Justine.

'Ah, no, no, he had assistants taking pictures for him.'

That is how busy Panokromatic Studios was. Everyone in the township wanted their photo taken. Now, as the old premises come into sight, I'm a little disappointed when Sekuru points to a block housing several small shops selling knick-knacks such as airtime and cell phone chargers. There is nothing except Sekuru's enthusiasm to suggest that this is where young Africans stole time away from work under baas or political organizing to line up to have their photo taken, many for the first, and perhaps only, time. The lackadaisical, almost indifferent energy of the young tuck-shop operators doing just enough to make ends meet pales against the energy Sekuru, walking stick in hand, has, as he seems momentarily to relive the days when he was the young, handsome bus conductor who brought his wife and children to come pose for Lovemore Mtema's assistants.

Sekuru lifts his walking stick to point to a yellow double-storey municipal building diagonally across from Panokromatic Studios.

'That used to be the office of Location Superintendent MacGregor.'

This office was the first port of call in the white man's town. It was Superintendent McGregor who registered entry and exit through a pass system of zvitupa, which your employer, the police, council workers – really any white person – could demand as identification. It was the Superintendent who allocated accommodation, who assigned children to schools, whose loudspeakers made announcements, summoned residents to his office and blasted propaganda from the Central African Broadcasting Service and later the Federation Broadcasting Corporation.

Against such heavy settler regulation of African life, the early 50s establishment of the Federation of Rhodesia and Nyasaland – today's Zimbabwe, Zambia and Malawi – briefly opened a window of hope that conditions might improve for Southern Rhodesia's black people. Instead, a new politics of racial 'partnership' was envisioned as a horse-and-rider relationship where Africans, predictably, were the mules of the settler state.

At the familial level, the Dzumbiras suffered the untimely death of their mother after a severe illness. As the oldest child, an adolescent Lilian, who had acquired a basic education at Sakubva School, took on much of the responsibilities of the home, mothering her young brother and their three other school-going siblings. 'She would speak once and you would listen,' Sekuru Justine says of his sister. 'But she was very fair. We loved our big sister very much.'

Sekuru Ifayi remarried five years later and had six more children. They continued to live at 264 until the end of their father's employment when he took up his blacksmith work at a new home in Dora Dombo Reserve.

Sekuru Justine recalls that around the time he was five years old and his sister was in her mid-teens, a motorbike began to come around the corner. 'We would hear the sound of the mudhudhudhu passing, and then Lily would make me accompany her out of the house, and we would go and see him. He would give me sweets so that I wouldn't tell them at home.'

The owner of the bike was a young man by the name of Kenneth Chigumadzi, my grandfather. With his Standard Three education from Goromonzi, the first government-run secondary school for Africans, he was fairly well educated. He had followed his father, Enos 'vaMupurisa' Chigumadzi, who was stationed at the Penhalonga Police Station, to the Eastern Highlands. Using his Standard Three report card, Kenneth secured respectable work as a mabharani, an accounts clerk, at the Rhodesian Duty Company in nearby Sakubva.

'Ha, vaChigumadzi loved to go to the kokotero.' These cocktail bars were an upmarket place where African 'ladies' and 'gentlemen', who were not allowed to drink 'European beer' and had to observe an evening curfew in the European town, could be served. If they were not at the beer-halls or the kokotero, entertainment could be found at the Native Recreation Hall. As we drive onto the outskirts of Sakubva, Sekuru Justine points to an old, yellow-painted hall, looking as if he is about to jump to his feet and dance, 'Uh-huh, at Beit Hall we used to go for mabioskop and maTin-Dance.'

It was not the respectable thing for a woman to do, but there were a few women performers at the time. Mbuya Lilian and her peers might have been especially provoked by Dorothy Masuka, the 'famous Rhodesian Stage Star' who, in 1956, sang about a beautiful girl named Nolishwa who wore trousers. In the song, concerned townsfolk report the surprising behaviour of Nolishwa whom they have seen just yesterday – *with another man, wearing trousers!* To their shock, Nolishwa's man replies that he loves her just as she is.

Sung in two voices, 'Nolishwa' pointed to the tug of war between the wills of African men and women in the urbanizing colony. In the 30s, some African patriarchs colluded with the colonial state to introduce passes restricting African women's movement in urban areas. African women nonetheless held their space in urban areas organizing campaigns such as the 1934 beer-hall boycotts on their own or alongside their male counterparts. In 1956, the year of 'Nolishwa''s release, African women living at Carter House hostel in Harare African township, now Mbare, were raped by male workers as 'punishment' for breaking the Salisbury Bus Boycott led by the newly formed City Youth League.

African women performers such as Dorothy Masuka sang in critique of both the settler state and the African patriarchs who appeared to agree with the Shona proverb, 'musha mukadzi', the home is the woman. The Union of South Africa's Prime Minister, Jan Smuts, declared that 'it is not white employment of native males that works the mischief, but the abandonment of the native tribal home by the women and children'. Both agreed that the threat of the 'urbanized detribalized natives' was best managed by fixing African women in the past, while African men could be trusted to negotiate the risks and rewards of chimanjemanje in the white man's town. The Nolishwas and other modern African women were often portrayed as prostitutes, known for their corrupting influence on African men and African society because they refused their places in time.

In the midst of all these pulls of will, Lilian Dzumbira stepped into the Panokromatic Studios and waited for her own mark on time to be taken. Lilian married young and had her first child when she was seventeen, so she was not the twenty-something-year-old I imagined her to have been in the photo. She must have been around sixteen years old when the photo was taken. 1956. Nolishwa's year. Perhaps she was alone or she had come with a friend or Kenneth, the handsome, bike-riding mhabarani courting her. Perhaps she had her own pair of trousers, perhaps she shunned them. Perhaps she was a 'good-time girl', perhaps a girl weighed down by family responsibility. Perhaps somewhere in between. Waiting for the flash of the camera directed by one of Lovemore Mtema's assistants, she projected a countenance beyond her years. A woman who, like her country, had and would continue to experience much turmoil in her life and yet would come out on the other side with a triumphant spirit, ready to stand tall and meet the world's gaze.

Kenneth was soon poached to work at Eastern Highlands Rhodesian Plantation, a tea estate in the nearby Honde Valley. He and Lilian moved into the marriage quarters of the plantation where they would have their first three children. In those years, Lilian's brother Justine and their only sister Miriam would often visit during school holidays; the young schoolboy was already being swept up in the unrest spreading across the colony.

As the broader political tensions in the country began to intensify, the usual Sunday pastimes were giving way to political rallies and meetings where as late nationalist leader Nathan Shamuyarira recalled, 'thudding drums, ululation and prayers to the ancestors began to feature more prominently'. In the inter-Chimurenga years, spiritual conquest left many turning to the missions, producing an elite Christian leadership. As Africans began questioning the effectiveness of mission Christianity in fighting their oppression, the 20s and 30s became the great founding age of independent African churches. While Sekuru Ifayi's family attended the Independent African Church, Umtali-born Johanne Maranke's Apostolic Faith movement spread in popularity across the country. The movement assumed indigenous religions' fundamental notions of healing, prophecy, and exorcism, and sung the great Africanist hymn, 'Ishe Komborera Africa', God Bless Africa, as it declared that salvation would come from Africans themselves.

By the late 50s, Africans drew more heavily on ancestral religions and tradition to imagine a new politics of self-liberation. If Mbuya Lilian and Sekuru Kenneth had been in Mbare's Stodart Hall, they may have seen a young former City Youth League leader, Robert Mugabe, sixteen years her senior and nine years his, who, at a ZANU conference, cast off his jacket, charging, 'If I must lose my freedom because of these so-called civilized clothes the white man brought, then he can have them back and I have my freedom!'

Far from being the bewildered tribesmen in white men's towns that the colonial authorities saw them as, Africans were staging a complex, and often contradictory, negotiation of chinyakare and chimanjemanje, the old and new, tradition and modernity, appropriating what worked for them and discarding what didn't. What would Kenneth and Lilian have thought as Mugabe declared, 'Today you have removed your shoes. Tomorrow you may be called upon to destroy them altogether or to perform other acts of self-denial'?

What the young Mugabe was hinting at was a struggle for the mastery over time in an era where Africans in the colony were wearing madhukwa, skin hats, along with their suits and greeting each other as vana wevhu, *children of the soil.*

In 1962, ninety-year-old First Chimurenga veteran Sekuru Nyamasoka Chinamhora powerfully bridged the gap between chinyakare and chimanjemanje when he travelled to Salisbury airport to present ZAPU president Joshua Nkomo, on his return from an overseas trip, and his colleagues with ritual weapons. In Chimurenga's intergenerational spirit, Sekuru Chinamhora instructed the young nationalists to 'Take this sword and these other weapons of war, and with them fight the enemy to the bitter end. Let the time be the same as those days when we used to keep as many cattle as we wanted. Also let it be that we shall plough wherever we like and as we like'.

In this way, time would be decolonized, the conflict between chinyakare and chimanjemanje resolved, with the return of Africans to the soil, and in turn, the soil to Africans.

Of that same year, in which the Federation's general elections were to be held, Sekuru Justine recalls, 'The whole of 1962, no one went to school. We were Nkomo's zhandas. We would hit out streetlights and cause disorder.' The following year, the short-lived Federation of Rhodesia and Nyasaland collapsed. Tensions in ZAPU split the party into the Ndabaningi Sithole-led ZANU, which would become increasingly Shona dominated, and the Joshua Nkomo faction, which grew to draw from a largely Ndebele-speaking constituency. By 1964, the year that Mbuya Lilian's third child, my father, was born, Mugabe and other nationalist leaders would be detained. On 11 November 1965, at 1.15 p.m., the newly elected Prime Minister Ian Smith broadcast a pre-recorded statement on the Rhodesia Broadcasting Corporation announcing the Unilateral Declaration of Independence from Britain for its insistence on 'NIBMAR', No Independence Before Majority Rule. A state of emergency clamping down on the social lives of Africans in townships, banning them from gathering in groups, no matter how small, no matter the cause, was declared. Blacks would never rule in his lifetime. Smith swore to it.

A s the Unilateral Declaration of Independence (UDI) came into effect in the mid-60s, Kenneth, who was forced to leave the tea estate after a long and severe illness, found employment at African Marketing Services' Salisbury city centre offices. The company secured him accommodation in a succession of the city's townships: Glen Norah, then to the adjacent Mufakose and Highfield. All of these political hotbeds for the nationalist movement which had begun to sabotage the Rhodesian state in attacks such as Chinhoyi in 1966 and Hwange in 1967, before waging a protracted struggle in the early 70s.

By the time my father began primary school in 1970, Mbuya Chigumadzi lived in Murehwa communal lands. As the flames of Chimurenga were being stoked in the countryside, it was here that she raised my father and his four siblings. Though my grandfather did the best he could, being away from each other was difficult, especially as several family crises came her way. As the war 'became hot', Mbuya Lilian's mother-in-law Mbuya Rophina would often be the point of convergence for comrades requiring food and other supplies to be organized from the village. Along with other village women, they provided the comrades with support whilst trying to protect their young children from recruiters on both sides. They continued this work, typical of the central role rural women played in supporting the war effort, until ceasefire was called in 1979.

In 1978, the town council of the new township of Chitungwiza recruited Sekuru Kenneth. It was here that he died in a car accident four years later. Despite patriarchal traditions around widowhood, such as kugara nhaka, the practice of inheriting a deceased brother's family and property, my grandmother Lilian insisted on remaining in Murehwa with her young children without remarrying, even as a young widow, and continued to insist on Murehwa as her inherited musha. From here, with the resourcefulness of the many rural women who keep their families together even as circumstances try to pull them apart, she continued to provide her children with a home and, as she proudly let people know in her later years, sent them to school through the work of her hands. Supplementing her husband's pension and his parents' assistance with what she earned from her farming and knitting, she clothed, fed and educated her children. Mbuya remained with this restless spirit until the end of her life on 6 October 2017.

I wept for not having the privilege to be among the hundreds-strong celebrants gathered at her funeral. I wept for the lost photo. I wept even more for the unanswered questions containing a history that was surely lost to me for ever.

I wondered, what story would Mbuya have written of her life? Would Mbuya have recognized the young woman who had stepped into Panokromatic Studios? Would the young woman have recognized the seventy-seven-year-old woman laid to rest, as per her wish, in the yard of their homestead in her red and white Mothers' Union uniform? What would Mbuya, who had an unfailingly sharp tongue, have said about the sixty-odd intervening years of her life? A life in which each loss and disappointment presented an opportunity but also pulled from within her greater depths of her spirit?

V

On 15 August 1991, my mother gave birth to me at the Mbuya Nehanda maternity ward of Parirenyatwa, Zimbabwe's largest hospital. Although it is a birthplace I share with tens of thousands of others, I grew up thinking of it as auspicious.

How fortunate was I to be born in a place named after the most famous person in Zimbabwe's liberation history? A political leader who defied expectations of African women's place in history by leading men and women in an anti-colonial war. A military tactician who is remembered in popular mythology for commanding, 'Tora gidi uzvitonge.' Take the gun and liberate yourself. A spiritual leader who held to her beliefs and refused to the end to convert to Christianity. A visionary who is immortalized through her famous dying words, uttered as she faced execution for her role in the First Chimurenga, 'My bones will rise again.'

How can I not be proud of this birthplace, when I have seen Mbuya Nehanda's restless spirit carried by many women, big and little? My grandmother Mbuya Lilian Chigumadzi, one of them. How telling is it that the word mbuya, or ambuya, refers to both grandmother and spiritual woman?

Having moved to South Africa in 1994, the year of its first democratic elections, I am a 'born-free' of Southern Africa's two dominant former settler colonies. The thrusting of this title on the young by the old is part of an understandable desire to be free of their past, as if the mere passage of time will erase the injustices of the past. To grow up in the body of a young black woman moving between Zimbabwe's post-independence and South Africa's post-apartheid eras is to understand that time does not erase that history, and so I seek guidance from these mbuyas who have led men and women in ways big and small, ahead of their time, defiant of the body's limits.

Like many other Zimbabweans, long before I knew much of the histories Mbuya Nehanda's spirit has possessed, I knew her name and her image. Beyond the once-obligatory portraits of an ever-youthful President Robert Mugabe, there is perhaps no image that is more recognizable than the famous photograph of Mbuya Nehanda and Sekuru Kaguvi's First Chimurenga mediums. The photograph, which the late novelist Yvonne Vera named the 'frozen image', would become an infinitely reproducible symbol of national pride and sovereignty, whether placed above the head of Robert Mugabe and an image of Great Zimbabwe in an early 80s ZANU–PF Independence-Day poster or as the inspiration for a bronze sculpture alongside Sekuru Kaguvi in the Zimbabwe Parliament.

In 1898, the British South Africa Police captured the 'frozen image' of Nehanda and Kaguvi standing in front of a Salisbury jail's brick wall, their shadows looming, as they await execution: 'Nianda' convicted for the murder of Henry Pollard, Native Commissioner for Mazowe; 'Kagubi' for the murder of an African policeman and messenger named Charlie. On the right, Sekuru Kaguvi stands awkwardly apart from the wall, his back bent, arms slightly akimbo. He appears wary, perhaps contemplating his eventual capitulation: agreeing to being baptized and named Dismus – the thief saved by Jesus. On the left, Mbuya Nehanda leans against the wall, her hands clasped firmly in front of her. She appears resolute, defiant, her eyes narrowed into an oppositional gaze, refusing to accept responsibility for the murder of that troublesome European the Africans knew as Kunyaira. With this 'mug shot', the settlers mocked the Africans, 'Where is the spirit now?'

In a spiritual tradition that believes the ancestors live on, watching over the living, the belief in vadzimu holds that ancestral spirits can choose to return, in times of family or national crisis, through living mediums. Nehanda, a royal ancestral spirit, is one who has come back again and again, answering the needs of the children of the soil, the descendants she watches over.

In the oral tradition related to me by mbira musician Ambuya Stella Chiweshe, Nehanda was among the first ancestors of the Shona who came from Guruuswa, literally the 'Tall Grass', in what is now Central East Africa's Great Lakes region. In other traditions, the spirit was the daughter of Mutota, the founder of the Mwenemutapa Dynasty, who was ordered to commit ritual incest with her brother in order to consolidate his empire's power in the fifteenth century. What all of the numerous varying origin stories agree is that Mbuya Nehanda is a founding ancestor spirit, an owner and custodian of the land who has possessed various spirit mediums over many centuries.

During the First Chimurenga of 1897–98, the spirit of Nehanda possessed a woman by the name of Charwe living in North-western Zimbabwe's Mazowe Valley. After rebellion began in Matabeleland in March 1896, it spread to Mashonaland by June, as they were joined by Mupfure Valley leader Mashayamombe, who worked alongside Kaguvi and later, Mazoe Valley leader Hwata, who collaborated with Nehanda. In the Chimurenga of the 70s, Mbuya Nehanda's spirit was carried by a woman named Mazviona, living in Dande Valley. Supported by three other spirit mediums – Chidyamauyu, Chipfene and

Chiodzamamera – Nehanda provided moral authority and guidance to the liberation movement's guerrillas fighting against the Rhodesians.

A few days after our visit to the photographic studio in Sakubva to track down the image of Mbuya Lilian, my maternal uncle Ben Chiganze and I set off for Dande Valley. Mazviona, Mbuya Nehanda's medium, has long since passed and so we are in search of a person who knew her well, one who acted as her spiritual aide during the war. This is Rogers Kayerenga, the spirit medium of Chidyamauyu.

A s you drive the 230 km due north-west of Harare, you realize that although Dande isn't very far in terms of distance, its existence is far removed from the life of the capital. If Harare, with its long history of colonial interaction, represents the modernity of chimanjemanje, Dande, which had survived much of the colonial ordeal because of its inhospitable climate and terrain, represents the tradition of chinyakare. Time and not mileage is the real distance between the two. Even if it is the first time you have visited, you do not go to Dande, you return to it.

And perhaps because of this, Dande has gained a cultural mystique as the spiritual home for all. It is a rite of passage for any mbira-playing or mbira-inspired musician to 'return' to Dande. Stella Chiweshe, Ephat Mujuru, Thomas Mapfumo, Oliver Mtukudzi and even the relative newcomer Jah Prayzah are among those who have paid homage to the ancient valley. When I mention that I am going to Dande, people nod in appreciation, 'Ah, Dande? Kumusha kwaMtukudzi.' Not only are Oliver Mtukudzi's people from Dande, but his totem, Nzou Samanyanga, Elephant, keeper of the tusks, is that of the region's royal clan. By far the most popular ode to Dande is Mtukudzi's 'Dzoka Uyamwe', 'Come Back and Suckle', a song of longing and homecoming. A person shunned by a world that sees the darkness of their skin as an indication of a bad soul cries out for home. In response, Mother beckons them to come. The place you left is still here. My breast is waiting for you. Dzoka uyamwe.

After their crushing initial defeat by the Rhodesian state, the liberation movement abandoned the strategy of isolated attacks such as Chinhoyi in 1966 and 'returned' their struggle to Dande. By 1971 the guerrilla forces of ZANU's military wing had penetrated the valley in order to politicize its people and recruit fighters. The movement's leaders had realized that the war for liberation could not be won without it being 'given to the people', especially those residing in the country's rural areas. Recognizing the need for a new mode of protracted struggle that required a different kind of moral and cultural authority, Dande, the home of Mazviona, the woman possessed by Mbuya Nehanda's spirit, became one of the first operational zones that the liberation movement opened in Zimbabwe.

Even after handing the decapitated heads of Mbuya Nehanda and other First Chimurenga leaders to Queen Victoria, the Rhodesians knew that they had not managed to crush the Africans' spirit of resistance. They may have taken claim over the land on which Africans lived, but they had not conquered nyikadzimu, the spiritual realm in which our ancestors, who had time and again fought for our land's protection, resided. Even as the Rhodesians appointed indigenous leaders they imagined they could control, the power of the ancestral spirits, returning through their mediums, was understood by all in the country. And even as the Rhodesians attempted to recruit their own mediums to speak against the call for the land's return, the true authority was with the spirits called upon by the children of the soil, the freedom fighters. And they called upon Nehanda's spirit to help them fight once again. With this alliance, Zimbabwe's past, present and future were unified in the latest struggle for self-liberation.

Around 40 km into our return to Dande, my uncle points ahead to the lush green fields, thickly wooded forests and deep red rich soil of the Mazowe Valley: 'This is Gracelands.'

Vast tracts of prime agricultural land belonging to a single large-scale farmer, former First Lady Grace Mugabe, stretch ahead of us. It is not just the land, famous for its citrus plantations, that has been approbated to a kingdom belonging to a First Lady and a President who, ironically, had preached 'one person, one farm'. To our right is the Mazowe Dam, which she had closed off to the rowing and fishing and other recreational activities that had once made it a popular local destination to the public. A site across the dam was earmarked for her legacy project, Robert Mugabe University. A few kilometres down the winding road, we pass the large cream-coloured wall surrounding the impressive campus of her private school on our right. To our left is a billboard giving directions to the offices of Gushungo Industries, named for former President Mugabe's clan name.

Driving through Gracelands, I am reminded that in December, as we returned from visiting our family kumusha and drove through the agricultural town of Marondera, Oliver Mtukudzi's 'Murimi Munhu' (literally 'A Farmer is a Human Being') played for the second time in twelve hours on a local radio station as we passed a billboard which declared to motorists and pedestrians, 'Kohwai pakuru!' 'Reap a plentiful harvest!'

After years of difficulty, agricultural productivity levels are rising, in many cases approaching pre-land-reform levels, as smallholder farmers like the one on the billboard and the family members we visited are gaining expertise and experience. The song felt fitting for this time. Murimi munhu. Those who till the land embody our humanity, embody our nation's hope.

When the song was released back in 2001, fast-track land reform was taking place. Understandably, there were many questions around Tuku's message. Who was, or is, the farmer Tuku refers to?

To understand the complexity behind Tuku's assertion that 'a farmer is a human being', you would need to know what is meant when a person asks the question: 'Munhu here?' Is this a human being? It's a question in keeping with what the Shona know as hunhu, and what is popularly known by its Zulu equivalent, ubuntu. This is the philosophy of Bantu-language speakers across Southern Africa, best understood by the aphorism 'a person is a person through others'. It is a philosophy of ethical personhood that leads many of our mothers and fathers to reprimand us for bad behaviour, especially in the company of others, by demanding to know 'Kuita kwemunhu here?' Is this how human beings behave? It's a question that can also be levelled towards a group of people in light of their history of actions with Africans. Given white settlers' unjust conquest of land and indigenous people, it is possible that when wanting to know the race of a person you can ask, 'Munhu here?' and, should the person be white, it is appropriate to answer, 'Aiwa, murungu.' No, they are a white person. In other words varungu, white settlers, have not been considered vanhu, people, because of their historic failure to treat the indigenous people with hunhu, humanity.

As we pass through the vast expanse of Gracelands, taken so wantonly and home to farm workers who often went unpaid, it becomes clear that these are certainly not the farmers we may think of as people embodying our humanity.

And that is not all there is to consider. Aware of the Mazowe Valley's spiritual significance as a home of Mbuya Nehanda's spirit, the then First Lady claimed this heritage at a rally held in the Mashonaland Central province town of Bindura a few months before the de facto coup thwarted her presidential ambitions:

> God said, 'Go and work in Mash Central'. Here... is where Mbuya Nehanda comes from. In that pit where I am based, for those who know history, that is where she was captured by the whites and then executed in Harare... as the wife of your leader, being allowed to build on such a place, I see it that I am representing Mbuya Nehanda.

The claim to mediumship is always complex, especially when the spirit is as revered and powerful as that of Mbuya Nehanda. The more powerful a spirit, the more likely it is to possess several mediums at the same time. What is important is that the spirit mediums are recognized by other established mediums. They will verify if the medium, among other things, possesses a deep historical knowledge of the people, the ancestral lineage and the land it protects; can perform ritual tasks such as retrieving or identifying specific items used by the spirit's previous medium and, importantly, conducts itself as a vessel fitting for the ancestral spirit it will carry. Importantly, as the holders of their people's values and traditions, the life of a medium by necessity is one of hardship, trial and strict observance of cultural practices and taboos.

And so, the claim by the former First Lady, someone so apparently divorced from the spiritual tradition that Mbuya Nehanda represents, is one that more than scandalized the public. If a deep sense of regard for the humanity of others is central to our spirituality, then the wanton appropriation of land and the abuse of farm workers, along with the former First Lady's extravagant lifestyle in the face of the country's poverty and her presidential campaign which was built on the public humiliation of others, makes the claim to holding Nehanda's spirit blasphemous indeed.

Once Gracelands is behind us, the road becomes fairly quiet. Our journey to the home of Chidyamauyu, spiritual aide to Nehanda as she guided the comrades during the Second Chimurenga, would be faster if we knew exactly where we were going. Thankfully, Chidyamauyu's name is well known in the Dande area and we are able to rely on the villagers' directions.

As we pass the rural town of Centenary, 145 km from Harare, we descend in altitude and begin to feel that we are going pasipenyika, to the bottom of the earth. Signage depicting elephants reminds us that this is a wilderness area. The temperature rises and the soil becomes poorer and the land more densely populated until we begin our ascent into the Mavuradonha mountains. The Dande Valley spreads out before us revealing land below which, except for the irrigated farmlands at the foot of the mountains, looks like a bed of grey-brown thorns.

Tattered Apostolic Faith church flags are planted in a significant number of homesteads. Unlike the rural areas I am used to visiting whose landscapes are dotted with neo-traditional homestead set-ups, typically with a grass-thatched brick kitchen and one or more dhanduru, the brick, four-corner dining room where families can either sit and listen to the radio, or sleep, most of the houses here are of mud and pole and only a few are built with brick.

In the past, Dande's Korekore people lived near the riverbanks which provided salt, their main trade from the sixteenth to the twentieth century. Now, we pass small goat and cattle herds here and there. The few crop fields are mostly cotton, sometimes maize wilting in the sun. Vanorarama nei? That is all I can think as we drive through the valley. How do they survive? There must be something, because, while there are certainly no potbellies, there are also no tell-tale kwashiorkor stomachs.

We pick up an old man who points us in the general direction of Chibaya village. On the instruction of a woman wearing the white robe of John Masowe's branch of the Apostolic Faith Church, we continue until we arrive at a T-junction. General dealers and a bus stop are to our right. We ask a young couple seated leisurely at the bus stop for Chidyamauyu and they point us to the homestead behind us.

We park in front of the homestead, prominent in its poor surroundings, with several structures including a bare brick kitchen, two separate living quarters, one structure with fading white paint and the other in a brown-yellow shade. It doesn't look like anyone is there.

I have forgotten my notebook so we decide to try the general dealers. Truthfully, I am nervous and this is helping me buy time. At the first store one 50-cent bond coin gets me two exercise books. On the store's cement counter are two-dollar plastic pumps in an assortment of colours and sizes. Aside from my flimsy slippers, I am wearing a knee-length wrap dress, a black dhukhu on my head and have an ankle-length zambia wrapped around my waist. To avoid offending the spiritual, I make sure not to buy the set of black-and-red patterned pumps. Red, I have learned, is taboo for its resemblance to blood.

I remember that I have been advised to bring a gift of bute. This storekeeper doesn't have any powdered tobacco. At the next store, a group of young men are gathered. It is different here in Dande, Sekuru Ben observed earlier, from other rural towns such as Beitbridge, Masvingo and much of Matabeleland which young men have deserted to try their luck in Botswana and South Africa. Clearly there must be something keeping them here. A few catcall me. Hearing my request, the storekeeper looks me up and down, before training his eyes on my dhukhu: 'Asi uri n'anga?' Instead of confirming whether I am a healer or not, I laugh and move on to other stores, none of which, it turns out, stock bute. On my return, I can already feel the sand burning my black plastic pumps, but I persevere. My uncle has managed to find out from the first storekeeper that Chidyamauyu passed on in 2005, but his wives are still alive.

At the homestead we ask the young woman who has come to greet us for the mother of the home. The woman, who looks to be in her early twenties, replies somewhat indignantly that it is she. We try again, saying we are looking for the wife of Chidyamauyu. 'She is here,' the woman nods before setting out. 'Tete!' The tete she is calling is his youngest widow, Mbuya Zvisineyi Maxine Kayerenga. She is in their fields, so she is not far. When she appears, Mbuya Kayerenga is relatively young, not more than sixty years old. The eldest of the three widows has gone away to visit family, the other appears not to live here anymore.

Mbuya Kayerenga invites us into her kitchen. It's an unexpectedly cool respite. Different from the ones we are used to in our part of the country, her kitchen seems a room more for dining and display, with polished walls carrying an arrangement of enamel dishes and clay pots and a central hearth, apparently not used for cooking, but rather to store drying dishes. Sekuru Ben sits on the cement bench running right round the circumference of the brick hut while I sit on a reed mat. Mbuya Kayerenga sits on the polished cement floor in front of me. She does not offer us water or anything to eat as she patiently waits for us to explain ourselves.

'My name is Panashe Chigumadzi. Kumusha kwangu ndekwaMurehwa. We are of the Shava clan. This is my sekuru, Ben Chiganze. Kumusha kwavo kuNyazura. He is of the Chihwa clan. We have come here to you because I would like to know nhoroondo reChimurenga. We have heard and read so many stories from the books, but we never get to hear it from the mouth of the source.'

'You want to know from me? I think there are others who know the history better than me.'

After all, as Mbuya Kayerenga later explains, she did not go to war herself, and she married her husband once he had come back after the 1979 cease-fire.

'That is fine, Mbuya. We will also go and speak to others, but we are happy to hear what you know about the Chimurenga, and your husband's involvement as a spirit medium.'

'Well, my husband was the "pocket" of the spirit of Sekuru Chidyamauyu. In flesh he was my husband; in spirit he was Chidyamauyu.'

The division between the medium and the spirit they embody is so blurred that Mbuya Kayerenga, like all those we have spoken to before coming to her home, refers to her late husband as 'Sekuru Chidyamauyu' or 'vaChidyamauyu', only revealing his name as Rogers Kayerenga when we ask for it much later in our conversation. A medium's physical identity is so inconsequential that at one spirit possession ceremony I attended the group of three female mediums were all referred to as 'Sekuru', because they were host to male spirits. Their gender did not matter because the medium is, after all, merely a bodily vessel submitting to the will of the spirit that has chosen them.

As is the case with those upon whom ancestral spirits descend, when the spirit of Chidyamauyu chose Rogers Kayerenga, a young man who had gone to mission school, he fell sick with a mysterious illness which no medicines could cure. Once a healer confirmed that a spirit had chosen to manifest itself through the young man, he would have had to undergo a ritual to identify the spirit before starting a long period of apprenticeship with established mediums.

In his everyday life, Chidyamauyu wore two lengths of black cloth, one tied around his waist and dropping to his ankles, the other draped over both shoulders and tied under his right armpit, as part of the many ritual practices and prohibitions he observed.

Mbuya Kayerenga explains that early in 1971 a small group of Zimbabwe African National Liberation Army (ZANLA) guerrillas led by commander Mayor Urimbo approached Sekuru Chidyamauyu and the mediums of Sekuru Chipfene and Sekuru Chiodzamamera. The guerrillas had crossed from Mozambique into Dande, initially approaching the people of the valley, who in turn said they should consult the mediums. Chidyamauyu and his colleagues led the comrades to Nehanda's ancient medium, a woman who maintained an austere material life, eating only ground-up food once or twice a week, apparently never bathing and who, it is said, 'hated European things'.

Mayor Urimbo and the comrades introduced themselves to Nehanda as 'children of Zimbabwe' who wanted to liberate the country from the colonial intruders. She agreed to help them in this struggle. Together, Nehanda and her fellow mediums endorsed the comrades to the people. Knowing the lay of the land well, Nehanda instructed the comrades on the best routes to take, where they were allowed to cross, sleep or fight, taught them to interpret the forest's signs so that they could avoid danger and know when their enemy was near, advised them on what kind of food to eat, and warned them to abstain from sex.

A few months after their arrival in Dande, the comrades began to fear that the ageing Nehanda would be captured and suffer the same fate of 'Nehanda aka dimburwa musoro nevarungu' – Nehanda who was beheaded by the whites at the turn of the century. The guerrillas carried the medium on a stretcher into Mozambique, eventually settling at the Chifombo camp on the Mozambique–Zambia border. As the youngest of her three spiritual aides, Chidyamauyu was responsible for the care of Nehanda and for conveying her instructions to the group. While in Chifombo, as the late Chidyamauyu put it, 'Vaititungamira muhondo yerusununguko.' She led us in the war of liberation.

'Before the medium died in 1973,' Mbuya Kayerenga tells us, 'her spirit told vaChidyamauyu that she is going to leave him to continue her work. She will give him the strength and guidance to continue.' The escalation of conflict made the spirit's instruction that her medium be laid to rest in Zimbabwe impossible. Instead, she was buried at a site en route from the Chifombo camp in Zambia.

The surviving spirit mediums did not return to Zimbabwe until the 1979 cease-fire. Alongside the many other indigenous and spiritual leaders who became close associates of the liberation movement, they continued to provide the skills, knowledge and moral authority that a 'people's war' required. It is, for example, common liberation lore that without the assistance of Chief Rekayi Tangwena and the mhondoro spirit he had called upon to guide and protect them through the difficult terrain of the Eastern Highlands, Mugabe, recently released from detention, and the late nationalist leader Edgar Tekere, may not have been able to cross safely from Zimbabwe into Mozambique to join the ZANLA guerrillas stationed at their main operational bases in 1975.

'After the war ended,' Mbuya Kayerenga says, 'they sent government officials to consult vaChidyamauyu on a few spiritual matters and that was it. It was never anyone senior.'

That Chidyamauyu no longer enjoyed the influence he had before the war does not seem to surprise his widow much, pointing to the fact that fewer and fewer people even here in the village of Chibaya seem to believe in ancestral religions and traditions. Young people in particular, she says, do not see the benefit of our ancestral religion. It hasn't, as they reason, really changed much for them here.

As far back as the early 80s, several spirit mediums in Dande began to complain of the government's neglect of the valley, warning that unless something was done, they would transfer their spiritual authority elsewhere. Since then, however, if there has been any dissent, it hasn't been able to deliver the province to which Dande belongs, Mashonaland Central, out of ZANU-PF's firm grasp.

I ask, 'Mbuya, given that Sekuru Chidyamauyu fought the war so that the land could be returned, did he benefit from land distribution in the 2000s?'

'We used to tell him about getting a farm, but he would refuse to go and beg for one.' She shakes her head, 'He would say, "I fought for the soil. They know what I did. I can't go around begging for a farm. They should come here and give it to me, in the same way they did with the house."'

The house Sekuru Chidyamauyu referred to is the small white structure we had seen outside which the government had built for him in the early 80s. The dilapidated house appeared to be the extent of patronage received by a man who, despite having abandoned all to support the liberation of the country as soon as it was asked of him, did not have the 'hero' status accorded to allies such as Chief Tangwena, famous helper of Mugabe, who was buried at the National Heroes' Acre in 1984, let alone his death honoured with any official attendance at his funeral.

Chidyamauyu's loyalty to Nehanda continued beyond independence, even if others forgot her once she was no longer useful. In 1982, two years after independence, Chidyamauyu led a group to recover Nehanda's bones from Zambia and rebury them in Zimbabwe, fulfilling the spirit's wish that her remains be returned to the soil of the ancestors.

Chidyamauyu's diminishing importance seems in part due to the fact that a new Nehanda had been found. A few weeks after my visit to his home, I would travel to Chikuti village, almost 20 km from the agricultural town of Karoi in north-east Zimbabwe, to see the large, security-guarded, government-sponsored shrine of a woman believed to be Nehanda in the post-independence period until her death a few years ago. It was here that the medium, who was reportedly involved in ZANU–PF party structures, was often consulted by members of the government and the army who, in turn, rewarded her with a farm.

Mbuya Kayerenga mentions the medium of Chikuti in passing as one of those who claimed Nehanda's spirit. Later she offers a familiar remark that seems to indicate that the spirit mediums of Dande did not recognize her mediumship: 'Since vaMazviona died, there has been no medium for Mbuya Nehanda. There have been many who claimed it, but they are not.'

'How do you know that they are not really possessed by Nehanda's spirit?'

'Ah, you will usually see that there will be much talk by people who claim to be Nehanda, but in the end it doesn't really go anywhere and the talk eventually dies down.' She continues, careful not to offer much detail, 'There is a little girl who we think might be Mbuya Nehanda, but we will see.'

Mbuya Kayerenga tells me that the young girl is the one who elders in the area have been speaking of for a few years. Observing and hearing of her behaviour and the supernatural things that seem to happen around her, they recognize the potential for such a powerful spirit to manifest in her. They are hopeful that Mbuya Nehanda will return, but they are in no rush to thrust this on the young girl just yet. It is important to wait to ensure that the child is indeed the vessel the ancient spirit has chosen. And if so, it is necessary to allow time for her to gain enough strength and maturity to carry all the weight that Mbuya Nehanda's spirit brings.

As we round out our conversation, Mbuya Kayerenga reminds us that there are others who know better, who know more about this history. All three of the spirit mediums – Chidyamauyu, Chiodzamamera and Chipfene – who travelled with Mbuya Nehanda during the war have died, but she refers us to Sekuru Chipfene's widow, Mai Chikara, who, Mbuya Kayerenga assures us, would definitely know more because she went to the war too.

Just before we leave, we take pictures of Mbuya Kayerenga outside her kitchen. At first she is reluctant but she soon relaxes and begins to enjoy herself as I show her how beautifully the images, especially the ones taken in front of her bougainvillea vines, are coming out. She begins to relay the stories of the many researchers, historians and colonial authorities who tried, and failed, to take pictures of Mazviona, the medium of Nehanda.

'She would simply say go ahead and take it, knowing that they would not reach wherever they were going back to.' She laughs, 'And it's true, despite all the attempts, there is not a single person with a picture of vaMazviona.'

We find the homestead of Mai Chikara almost 30 minutes away in the village of Chimoio, near the Msengezi River, a few hours' walk to the Mozambique border. With many bare and plastered brick structures, it appears to be more affluent than the Kayerenga's musha. Sekuru Ben and I make the mistake of entering the large compound through an opening adjacent to a sizeable cattle kraal. A small woman appears and points to make us go back, 'Who told you to come this way? Go through the front entrance.'

Although it is not immediately clear where the entrance is, we think it best not to argue and instead look around us. Once we are through the correct entrance, the woman, who looks to be in her early fifties, reappears. She introduces herself as Mai Chikara and promptly leads us into her kitchen. It is also cool, with a design similar to that of Mbuya Kayerenga, albeit with a more elaborate crockery display. I spot a photograph of a man, from the waist up, wearing the black cloth of a spirit medium. I attempt to sit on the floor but Mai Chikara refuses this and pulls me up to the bench where she herself sits. We exchange small talk about the lack of rain. Without being summoned, a young woman enters the kitchen offering us water followed by big mugs of maheu, a fermented maize meal drink which I have never particularly liked. They are clearly accustomed to hosting visitors. We have just eaten, so Sekuru Ben accepts the water and politely declines the maheu. Although I'm full, I'm aware of our awkward initial interaction and accept both in an attempt to ingratiate myself.

Mai Chikara ends the pleasantries and asks who we are and what our business here is. As we explain that we are researching the history of the Second Chimurenga, Mai Chikara narrows her eyes, stiffens her body and abruptly interrupts.

'Who told you that you would find me here? Did you go to the MP's office first?'

We let her know that after reading of Sekuru

Chidyamauyu in books and newspapers, we set out for the district and asked for directions to his home along the way. It was his wife Mbuya Zvisineyi Kayerenga who suggested we pay her a visit. Mai Chikara is not satisfied. She pulls out a small cell phone from underneath her top. She informs two 'comrades' and the district of Muzarabani's Member of Parliament of the presence of 'Comrade Ben Chiganze' and 'Comrade Panashe Chigumadzi' who are requesting an interview about her experience of the Chimurenga and requests their presence in dealing with the matter. One of the comrades is in hospital and cannot make it. The other, a lanky, middle-aged man, wearing an old black dress shirt, trousers and worse-for-wear slip-ons, soon arrives to join Mai Chikara on her interrogation bench.

Among the many questions the two comrades ask is what I will give them once my work is published. It is a fair question. I try my best to explain that the type of work I do is not usually particularly well rewarded. They fold their arms, unsatisfied. I am then requested to explain myself to Comrade MP Alfred Mufunga on the phone. I make my case. He doesn't talk much. He politely cuts me off and asks to speak to Mai Chikara. She relays the message: 'MP Mufunga says you should come tomorrow to introduce yourselves and your matter at the district meeting.'

In Sekuru Chipfene's wife, Mai Chikara, we are clearly dealing with munhu we musangano, a human being of the party. Along with Mbuya Nehanda of the Chikuti shrine, the Chipfene family seem to be among those who had been able to negotiate and benefit from the more material world of party politics once independence came. This is unlike the Chidyamauyu family who appear to have lost significance because of their insistence on focusing on spiritual matters. After the war ended and the nationalists came into power, the spiritual gave way to the material. Chidyamauyu embodied a 'post-Chimurenga' collapse of the partnership between the liberation movement and certain spirit mediums. The once crucial spiritual-political alliance broke down so that those spiritual leaders who could not, or would not, negotiate party politics and bureaucracy, have been marginalized. Those spiritual leaders who could manage the political game have been able to maintain their relevance and have apparently reaped the material rewards as Mbuya Nehanda of Chikuti did with her impressive state-sponsored shrine and farm, and Mai Chikara with her relatively affluent compound. And so, as a 'comrade', Mai Chikara is adamant in maintaining the protocol of only speaking on matters of the war with those who have the clearance of authorities higher than her own. We will not ambush this comrade into an unauthorized account of the Chimurenga. We should have called or gone to the office of the MP first before coming. The MP or one of his delegates would then have escorted us to their homestead.

'If you had done that, we could have told you enough to finish books like this,' the comrade gestures to his waist. 'With things like that, we cannot just talk. It needs others to be there and to have known beforehand.'

We let them know it will be difficult to come again tomorrow, but we will try another time. The two comrades turn to themselves and begin talking animatedly of their own affairs, paying no attention to me during my twenty-minute struggle to finish the jhompi of maheu.

VI

It begins to rain heavily as Sekuru Ben and I leave for Harare. I have a headache and am tired and frustrated. As I turn over Mbuya Kayerenga's doubtfulness and Mai Chikara's militance, I remember Mbuya Chiganze's words: 'Zvimwe hazvibvunzwe.' Some things are just not asked about.

Equally, some things are simply a matter of asking. At times, it feels that the more I hear, the less I know. I have found myself frustrated and even exasperated by the many meandering and often contradictory histories of Nehanda that I have heard when consulting spirit mediums, traditionalists and books, making it feel as if the single version of Nehanda that I initially tried to grasp, the one captured by the 'frozen image' of the medium who died while speaking her truth to the British settlers, is constantly slipping through my fingers like water.

When the frustration subsides, I'm struck by the narration of the long and complex history of a spirit who, in many accounts, has existed since the beginning of time, centuries before the coming of the British, and for that matter, the Portuguese and the Arabs. That is not the history I grew up with. I have to ask why we insist on reducing Mbuya Nehanda's spirit to the British colonial encounter as if she is only a spirit of yesterday?

Perhaps there is something to why Mazviona, Mbuya Nehanda's Dande medium in the Second Chimurenga, did not want to have her own picture out in the world. Perhaps she understood the complex manipulations her image would be subjected to in the struggles over time and national belonging.

Mugabe himself hinted at an answer when, after ZANU's victory over ZAPU in the first democratic elections of 1980, he declared, 'Independence will bestow on us a new... perspective, and indeed, a new history and a new past.'

In this new history of liberated Zimbabwe, the insistence on the version of Nehanda who was uncompromising and defiant right until the end masks the fact that the Second Chimurenga was ended through compromise. After all, shortly after the 1979 cease-fire, Britain brokered a negotiated settlement at Lancaster House in London, in which the Rhodesian minority government agreed to hand over political control to the black majority in return for their economic interests being secured by a constitution that protected their property rights. In the end, ZANU came into power in 1980 not through the barrel of the gun but through the ballot box.

In time it became clear that in this 'unified' Zimbabwe, some people were more Zimbabwean than others. Mbuya Nehanda's image was used to serve new and old ideas about who really belongs to and fought for Zimbabwe. If Zimbabwe is the spirit-nation exclusively belonging to Shona ancestors such as Nehanda and Kaguvi, then it follows that their Shona descendants are the true owners of the land. If Mbuya Nehanda authorizes a liberation narrative where Shona people are the key protagonists of anti-colonial resistance, the Shona-led First Chimurenga of 1896-97 towers over the Ndebele 1893 and 1896 wars. In this history, the Second Chimurenga was won by the Shona-dominated ZANU guerrillas with little real contribution from ZAPU's largely Ndebele-speaking military wing, meaning that independence really belongs to Shona people because they fought hardest for it. Never mind the fact that 'Shona-ness' is not a stable historical fact. This new Shona-centric history takes on the essentialism of colonial history, simplifying and exaggerating conflicts between different groups, papering over the complex ways in which African identity was continuously made and remade as peoples constantly migrated, inter-married, fought with and made peace with each other over time. What do we make of the fact that I, as a Shona-speaking person of the Shava clan, share the same eland totem with the Ndebele-speaking Mpofu clan? Never mind that, with the exception of the Khumalo clan, most of today's Ndebele speakers do not have Nguni ancestors but have 'Shona' ancestors. Or that many Shona people including my own Mbuya Chigumadzi and her family claim Nguni ancestors such as Dhliwayo and Zwangendaba Jele. Who, then, is really 'Ndebele' and really 'Shona'? Who is the true child of the soil?

This new history allowed for a ZANU-sponsored Shona hegemony in 'unified' Zimbabwe, fomenting the inhumane ways in which the post-independence government suppressed dissidence arising out of conflicts between the former ZANU, ZAPU and Rhodesian armies through an operation named Gukurahundi, 'the first rains that wash away the chaff'. Following the 1982 discovery of large arms caches in Matabeleland, the Korean-trained Fifth Brigade of the Zimbabwean armed forces enacted a series of massacres claiming the lives of more than 20,000 Ndebele people. Most of Gukurahundi's victims were civilians marked out and hunted as ZAPU 'dissidents' by the majority-Shona ZANU–PF government of Robert Mugabe. The post-independence government framed Gukurahundi, of which the de facto coup winner President Emmerson Mnangagwa was a key figure as then Minister of State Security, as an act of 'self-defence' on the part of the 'Zimbabwean people'. The campaign officially ended in 1987 when ZAPU leader Joshua Nkomo was cornered into signing the Unity Accord and dissolving his party into the 'new' ZANU–Patriotic Front (ZANU–PF), heightening those who were persecuted's awareness of their 'Ndebele-ness'. Memories of Gukurahundi and a continued second-class status have pushed some Ndebele into radical separatist movements, as other groups rail for a 'New Zimbabwe', inclusive of all citizens.

In the new history of Zimbabwe, it is not only the Shona who are singular in their contribution to the Chimurenga, it is men. Existing in the same era as Mbuya Nehanda's First Chimurenga spirit medium was Indlovukazi Lozikeyi Dlodlo, the 'Last King' of the Ndebele, who secretly led their resistance. Following Dlodlo were the many urban women campaigners, the rural women who bore the brunt of the liberation war crossfires, chimbwido collaborators cooking, cleaning and on the lookout for the comrades, and women political leaders and combatants who fought alongside their male counterparts. Mbuya Nehanda was not nearly as singular a woman in her spirit of anti-colonial defiance. So why do we insist on isolating her from other women? Entire histories of women's resistance in rural areas, cities, mines and farms before, during and beyond the Chimurengas are foreclosed by the singularity of Mbuya Nehanda's 'frozen image'.

Is fixing Mbuya Nehanda into the past something to do with an old nationalist fear about African women and their place in time? A fear that if we allow these women their full history, then they might become too troublesome and demanding in the future? A year after passing the historic 1982 Legal Age of Majority Act granting women majority status at the age of eighteen, the government embarked on Operation Clean Up, in which soldiers and police were deployed to clear Zimbabwe's urban centres of women who had the temerity to be unaccompanied in public after nightfall, arresting them on the charge of being 'prostitutes'. This at a time when Mbuya Nehanda was symbolically domesticated as Mother of the Nation, Womb of the Nation, through the naming of the nation's largest maternity ward after her. Decades after independence, the charge of 'prostitution' has continued to be used to discredit female politicians.

From the late 90s, Mbuya Nehanda increasingly became the centrepiece of ZANU-PF's rediscovered revolutionary politics, as it was threatened by a rioting labour movement and civil society protesting structural adjustment policies, and war veterans demanding compensation, including pensions and the land they had fought for. Obscuring ZANU's own genesis as an urban movement, the ruling party appropriated old colonial ideas to create a new post-independence politics of time and space, presenting their rural support base as 'authentic' traditional people who had known Chimurenga, and the newly formed Movement for Democratic Change's urban support base as 'inauthentic' sell-outs and Western puppets who did not understand or experience the Chimurenga.

Having appropriated the war veterans' legitimate demand for land, Mugabe, following in the spiritual lineage of royal guardians of the land such as Mbuya Nehanda, provided political and spiritual leadership of this 'Third Chimurenga' of the 2000s. In a complex management of time, ZANU-PF 'inappropriated the now', so that present struggles were a necessary sacrifice to the fulfilment of a revolutionary future which was a re-articulation of a glorious African past.

Almost eighteen years after the Third Chimurenga began, it was in the name of revolution that the military took over the country from Mugabe, the ageing Father of the Nation, whom they claimed was being misled by his wife Grace, an ambitious younger woman, branded as clinically ill and, that old term for troublesome women, a prostitute. With army tanks behind them, citizens chanted, 'Hatitongwe nehure'. We won't be ruled by a whore.

In this military-assisted transition, Mbuya Nehanda's 'frozen image' has something to tell us about the centrality of violence in the making and remaking of Zimbabwe. Understandably, after a liberation war that claimed as many as 80,000 lives, it is often said that 'Zimbabwe yakauya neropa.' Zimbabwe came into being through blood. Added to that are the uncounted lives lost in the inter-Chimurenga years, those lost in the First Chimurenga and the many more lost before that. Perhaps because of this we defy our own belief in the timelessness of Nehanda's spirit and remain fixated on the frozen image of her medium facing imminent death. It is as if the moment of the spirit medium's execution is the moment of Zimbabwe's birth. Is our fixation with Nehanda's death a cathartic confrontation of our colonial trauma? Or is it an acceptance of violence as being always necessary in our making and remaking? Perhaps we continue to rehearse Nehanda's execution because we have not found the way to resolve the traumas of our violent past and present?

Are these even the right questions to ask?

In my search for answers and questions, many spirit mediums through whom the ancestors speak and return to guide the soil, guardians of a culture that is against kuteura ropa, the shedding of blood, have expressed extreme displeasure at violence, going as far as to shun the colour red. Our traditional belief systems sanction violence only in extreme circumstances, and even then the community as a whole must account for the bloodshed. If you do not account for wrongful death, you and your descendants will continue to be haunted by ngozi, the restless and malevolent spirit of a person whose life was cut short. Asked about the fate of our nation and her people, several spirit mediums I have spoken to tell of the need for ritual-ceremonies to cleanse the land and the people of the Chimurengas' bloodshed and trauma. Our constant return to the image of Mbuya Nehanda's imminent execution is a sign that our nation is being haunted by the spirits of all those whose blood has been shed in the series of violent clashes that continue to make and remake Zimbabwe.

VII

'Ridza hako, Jah Prayzah!'

The presidential inauguration's master of ceremonies, Advocate Jacob Francis Mudenda, adopts a jovial tone as he bids the country's most popular musician to go on and do his thing, play one of his hits.

As I watch the inauguration on my phone's screen, it feels a farcical gesture – a jester bidding the artist go on and entertain the court – that, I suppose, is as real as the seeming unreality that we have been made a part of over the last nineteen days. 6 November 2017, Mugabe fires then-Vice-President Emmerson Mnangagwa from his position. 13 November, head of the Zimbabwe National Army General Chiwenga denounces Mnangagwa's removal and declares that the army is prepared to defend the revolution and end the purges within ZANU–PF. 14 November, military tanks are seen rolling in on the outskirts of Harare. 15 November, the army takes over key state institutions and places Mugabe under house arrest. 18 November, a solidarity march, organized by the Zimbabwe National Liberation War Veterans Association and backed by the army, draws in citizens and opposition parties in their call for Mugabe's removal. 19 November, ZANU–PF removes Mugabe as their leader. 21 November, Mugabe tenders his resignation to parliament. It is now 24 November and, whether we believe it or not, we are witnessing the closing act of the fourteen-day political drama that had scripted in a swift and near-bloodless military takeover, the toppling of Robert Mugabe and now the swearing in of Emmerson Dambudzo Mnangagwa as the country's Head of State and Government and Commander-in-Chief of the Zimbabwe Defence Forces.

To be privy to this very public national theatre staged by the defence forces is the experience of a lifetime. One none had ever thought would happen. At twenty-six years old, I have known only Mugabe as the leader of Zimbabwe. With an opposition unable to outmanoeuvre ZANU–PF, Zimbabweans had long resigned any prospect of leadership change until Mugabe's death. Even then we weren't holding our breath for the ninety-three-year-old's demise. The late Morgan Tsvangirai's MDC, the largest opposition party, had never quite been able to live down the now-infamous 1999 image of white farmers queuing to cut cheques for the newly-formed party during a rally, nor has their inability to unite opposition successfully over the last seventeen years inspired confidence. Newer civil leaders such as Pastor Evan Mawarire of the #ThisFlag movement, Sten Zvorwadza of the National Vendors' Union of Zimbabwe and Promise Mkwananzi of Tajamuka/Sesjikile were able to re-energize an apathetic citizenry to stand up and declare what they were against, but weren't ultimately successful in achieving Mugabe's ouster.

Zimbabwean politics is a game of time and space and its manipulations. For all their moves and popularity, many found themselves sceptical of movements that also seemed unable to engage history and continued in the MDC's presentist tradition of pressing for a change seemingly undefined except for being an anti-Mugabe stance. Pressed, perhaps, by the urgency of economic hardship and the abuses of human rights that they rightly sought to ameliorate in the now, these movements seemed unable to articulate a vision of Zimbabwe's future that was well grounded in its past.

If ZANU-PF made the politics of now inappropriate, the opposition insisted on the present to the exclusion of the past. Where ZANU-PF's revolutionary closed fist kept an iron grip on the Chimurenga legacy, MDC's post-revolutionary open palm let it slip through its fingers.

In 2000, a few years into the MDC's establishment on the back of the labour movement, its late founding president Tsvangirai dismissed the war veterans in the midst of land reclamation as 'a bunch of outlaws'. With this, he displayed a lack of historical appreciation of the war veterans' post-independence neglect and how this made them manipulable by ZANU–PF. In reacting to Mugabe's positions on land, war veterans and the economy in ways like this, Tsvangirai's MDC effectively gave ZANU–PF the Chimurenga legacy on a silver platter.

ZANU–PF and its securocrats latched onto Tsvangirai's lack of a 'Chimurenga history', often warning 'hatingatongwe ne munhu asinakuenda kuhondo'. We can't be ruled by someone who did not go to war. Unfortunately, Tsvangirai, who instead of joining the comrades in Mozambique chose to continue supporting his family with his mineworker wages, seemed to buy into the narrative that the only way to have participated in the Chimurenga was to have carried a gun, and a ZANLA gun at that.

This exclusive version of history promoted a grave narrative injustice. Chimurenga is not ZANU–PF. The spirit of Chimurenga long precedes ZANU–PF and it will long outlive it. Chimurenga transcends time and space, belonging to our ancestors, our grandmothers, our mothers, ourselves and to our daughters and granddaughters. Instead of reclaiming Chimurenga for our people, our opposition conceded it to Big Men.

And indeed, in a political masterstroke, ZANU–PF, master manipulators of time that they are, has been able to appropriate the opposition's anti-Mugabe politics of change and neo-liberal policies, repackage them in terms of their Chimurenga politics and present them to us as the post-Mugabe 'Operation Restore Legacy'. Instead of a real revolution driven by the people and their own spirit of Chimurenga, we have had an internal coup where we, the people, have rubber-stamped a new military-backed neoliberal order.

Despite my deep-seated apprehension about this citizens' alliance with the military, on Saturday, 18 November 2017, the day of the Solidarity March in Harare, I drive with my cousin to a rally outside the Zimbabwean Consulate in Johannesburg, the city with the largest concentration of my country's diaspora. Singing, waving flags, holding banners, taking selfies and wearing national colours are hundreds of people, some here legally, some not, some eager to go home, some only hoping for relief for family back home. I see many friends and acquaintances from over the years, bubbling with a kind of nervous excitement only partially masked under the apathy many of us have come to wear as our default attitude.

'Ah, Panashe! You're here too? Come and see my daughter, she's also here!'

'Did you see Fadzi? She's behind that banner with her aunt.'

'Come and take a picture with me, I'm going to send it to my brother. They're on their way to State House.'

'Ha, this time, Panashe? This time, ka, I'm telling you the old man is gone.'

Tired of being told to 'go back home', of being called

'kwerekweres', of using fake names on fake papers, of cleaning people's homes instead of teaching, of being accused of stealing people's jobs, of stealing their women, of wiring money through Western Union, of queuing with a Munenzwa bus driver to send groceries or medicine to families back home, of being unable to attend the funerals of their loved ones, of being unable to see their children grow up, they shout 'Sokwanele!' 'Zvakwana!' 'It is enough!' railing as if a final heave of energy is all that is needed to push the old man out and all their dreams and aspirations, big and small, for their country in. For their children to find decent jobs, for their parents to be able to have pensions to retire on, for hospitals they can send their relatives to without the feeling they are sending them there to die, for national roads that do not risk their lives, for their speech to be free, for the lives of their family lost in Gukurahundi to be accounted for, for leaders who have won their respect and who they have chosen, for a place they can make a home of again.

For the rest of the 'Fourteen-Day Revolution', I'm glued to my phone and laptop. I have a TV, but have not had any network subscriptions for years. Even now I do not think to renew them, because international media, with its many mostly foreign white male 'Africa experts', is tiring. What is most grating are the remarks that the huge mass of citizenry working together with the army demonstrate what a 'peaceful coup' should look like, and better yet, how 'educated' and 'civilized' Zimbabweans really are. The boldest of them stop just short of openly attributing this to ninety years of British colonialism. The exception is our trusted Zimbabwean reporter, Haru Mutasa of Al-Jazeera English, but she makes frequent Twitter updates, so I don't have to tune in to the TV. I spend a lot of time scrolling through my Twitter timeline. In between, I call relatives and friends in Zimbabwe, but really Twitter knows everything before everyone else. WhatsApp is our undisputed public sphere connecting those at home with those in the diaspora. We share videos, screenshots of press statements, texts of news articles, broadcast links faster than anything on official media. With even more speed, we share memes, such as the Mugabes as destitute hitchhikers out of State House, and voice notes, such as those with people expertly switching between Mugabe's deep chiZezuru drawl and Queen's English, keeping us going with the humorous spirit Zimbabweans in and out of the country have long relied on to make it through hard times for all these years.

Keeping up with and cross-checking the daily reports, fake and accurate, soon becomes exhausting. I reach the end of my rope on Sunday, 19 November. Twitter says that a ZBC truck has been seen going in the direction of State House. World media informs us that Mugabe is going to announce his resignation on the national broadcaster this evening. This is probably the most anticipated speech in Mugabe's thirty-seven years of power. We, the viewing public, are effectively placed under house arrest. For whatever reason, when I receive the news of Mugabe's upcoming speech, I have just put a fifteen-minute leave-in conditioner in my hair. I get out of my bathroom and pull out my laptop to look for ZBC's Facebook link. Ad after ad appears. We wait. I still have the conditioner in my hair. Apparently the broadcast is being pre-recorded to ensure that the President will not veer from the agreed statement. My scalp is beginning to sting a little. When Mugabe does finally appear, he is flanked by the head of the Zimbabwe Defence Forces, General Constantino Chiwenga, and a number of other officials. This is not the ninety-three-year-old of tailored suits, shining skin and jet-black hair that we are used to, that preternatural reminder that if Mugabe could outmanoeuvre time and its efforts on his body, he was certainly going to outmanoeuvre, outlast and even outlive us all in the political game. Instead, this ninety-three-year-old looks dishevelled – hands dry, grey hairs uncharacteristically visible, perhaps confirmation of his rumoured hunger strike. Maybe, after all these years, time has finally cornered him?

Pages are pulled out. Mugabe subjects us to twenty minutes of meandering. He acknowledges the issues that the army has brought before him and then reassures all that he will officiate a ZANU–PF congress in December. At one point, he seems to put papers away, skipping over some parts. General Chiwenga behind him is visibly on edge. Just as we are waiting for him to mention his resignation, Mugabe, the cosmopolitan African liberation stalwart he is, lets us know that he has, after all, finished his speech, putting his papers down and thanking us for our time in Shona, Ndebele, Swahili and English: 'Tatenda, Ngiyabonga, Asante Sana. Thank you very much.' He's still sharp enough to understand that Africa and the world are watching him. It seems Mudhara has tricked us again. I close my laptop, log out of Twitter and get up to wash my over-processed hair. I no longer want to observe a political game I clearly do not understand.

Over the next two days, I allow myself to open links from WhatsApp now and then but mostly ignore my phone. I try to get back to the work I'd been neglecting over the past few days. I am happy to be informed of the results once this is over, whenever that will be.

On Tuesday, 21 November, feeling tired, I take a midday nap. Just over half an hour later I wake up to my WhatsApp buzzing with screenshots of Mugabe's resignation letter to the Speaker of Parliament. I am not sure what to do. I log on to Twitter. I scroll through the many updates filled with exclamation marks and crying face emoticons and Zimbabwean flags. Twitter says that Zimbabweans in Johannesburg's inner city of Hillbrow have taken to the streets. I wonder whether I should go there too. Something to do with 'being with the people' in this 'historical moment'.

I remain in bed, indecisive. I do not want to jump. I do not have tears of joy. Really, I am numb. I am not sure where this is going to take us.

I eventually call my mother. She is pensive too. When I tell her about the Hillbrow celebrations she cautions that the excitement and ensuing confusion may not be safe.

A Ndebele friend on a WhatsApp group questions how his fellow citizens can ask him to celebrate the ascension of a man who was instrumental in the murder of members of his family.

I go to bed with a headache.

In the midst of all the military pomp and fare staged at the National Sports Stadium, the MC Mudenda could not hide his enthusiasm for Jah Prayzah and had just stopped short of saying 'Go on and play, my son!'

This was warm encouragement from an uncle to a youthful son who had expressed a yearning for the return of his father. Jah Prayzah, whose real name is Mukudzei Mukombe, had fashioned himself as a son who had been 'foretelling' the coming of the ultimate father figure who would save the people from our misfortunes. In 2016 he released 'Mudhara Vachauya', The Old Man Will Come, which soon found itself at the centre of ZANU–PF succession wars. In Shona, to refer to 'mudhara', you mean to say, 'my old man' and in Zimbabwe's hierarchical society this can also refer to a powerful, usually older, man. Although Grace Mugabe's G40 (Generation 40) faction tried to counter-spin this popular song as an endorsement of Robert Mugabe, its reference to Shumba, Mnangagwa's lion totem, ensured his faction were the clear winners of the battle.

Long before 'foretelling' Mnangagwa's political ascendancy, Jah Prayzah had been courting the military. In a gesture he innocently describes as an ode to his childhood dream of becoming a soldier, he took to dressing his tall frame in military gear. Rather than censoring him, the Zimbabwe Defence Forces, which since independence has used music such as its own Military School of Music's hit single 'Mai vaDhikondo', Dhikondo's mother, a song reportedly used during and after the Gukurahundi killings to entertain and endear itself to the public, gave Jah Prayzah an 'ambassadorial role' with the aim of projecting 'a warmer, friendlier and more playful side'. A role which earns him the distinction of being the only civilian in the country allowed to wear a soldier's uniform.

This warmer, friendlier and more tactful side of the army was out in full force during the 18 November Solidarity March organized by the country's war veterans. In the giddy atmosphere of the 'fourteen-day Chimurenga', Jah Prayzah's military-beret-covered dreadlocks were perhaps the only thing that would distinguish him from the gun-toting soldiers seen kissing babies and taking selfies with a citizenry newly enamoured of their country's defence forces. The army's charm offensive worked, as citizens preferred the disciplined and courteous soldiers to the abusive and extortive police force who had made Zimbabwe's city streets and highways a nightmare.

By the end of the Solidarity March, these warm and friendly 'sojas' were the new 'baes' or 'Deddies' of the nation. 'Deddy' is what many people of a younger generation call our fathers, if we are not calling them by the more traditional term Baba. 'Deddy' is also a term for another type of man in your life – not a title for just any boyfriend or baby-father, it is reserved for a man who can *provide*. Circulating on social media is a meme of a gendered toilet sign in which 'Chiwenga' was graffitied over 'Men'. To use an Ndebele phrase Mugabe appropriated during the fast-track land reform, the nation's generals became the embodiment of amadoda sibili, real men. And that the sixty-one-year-old current Vice-President, former army head Constantino Chiwenga, has a young wife almost half his age makes the dream of every woman having her own 'Deddy Musoja' seem within grasp.

VIII

Each successive episode of Zimbabwe's Chimurengas requires, as Mugabe had said in 1980, 'a new... perspective, and indeed, a new history and a new past.' In the publicity tours that newly inaugurated President Mnangagwa undertakes in his first 100 days of office, he is careful to manage the narrative of our recent history. At a rally on 7 February 2018 in the rural town of Guruve, the president attempts to dispel the previous speaker, the ZANU–PF national political commissar's declaration that the military played a key role in Mnangagwa's ascension, saying instead that Mugabe 'realized that the people had spoken and the people's voice is the voice of God'.

In the history Mnangagwa has been crafting of 'Operation Restore Legacy', he is careful to present himself as the respectful and dutiful seventy-five-year-old son who merely took over the reins from a doting but ailing then ninety-three-year-old father who was being unfairly abused by a cruel stepmother and her cronies. In a pre-Davos dialogue with young Zimbabweans, Mnangagwa repeats a familiar refrain, saying 'to me he is my father, my mentor, my revolutionary leader... I am where I am today because for fifty-four years he has been holding my hand, but [because of his age] he was surrounded by what others described as criminals'.

It is into this, the more than decades-long political arena of father and sons, that the former First Lady, Grace Mugabe, had stepped. If we are a nation constantly searching for fathers, we are also looking for mothers who will make suitable helpmates for them.

As we have done with Mbuya Nehanda, the Mother of our Nation, the lone heroine of our Chimurengas, our political history is one that makes wombs of women, empties us of all human complexity, impregnates us with all that is good or wrong in our society so that women are either Mothers of the Nation, birthing all that is good, or Evil Stepmothers, birthing all that is bad in our society.

In a country where it is held as a dictum that 'musha mukadzi' – the home is the woman – Grace failed spectacularly where Mugabe's late first wife, Sally, dazzled. Sally's unassuming, soft-spoken nature and modest appearance are part of what endeared her to many Zimbabweans, who fondly called her 'Amai Sally', as the rightful helpmate to the father of our nation.

Having met him at a teacher-training college in her native Ghana, Sally Hayfron married Mugabe in 1961. She became increasingly involved in nationalist political causes in the 60s, leading campaigns for the release of Zimbabwean political prisoners whilst in exile, and for the safety and well-being of refugees of the Second Chimurenga whilst in Mozambique with her husband after his 1964 release. After independence, she became first lady to Zimbabwe's first black prime minister and was elected ZANU-PF Women's League secretary in 1989. Outside of politics, Sally continued to be popular for her involvement in welfare programmes such as the Zimbabwe Child Survival Movement.

This assignment of the role of Madonna to the first wife of the President, as with the singling out of Mbuya Nehanda, served a clear political purpose in the telling of history. It was not true that Amai Sally was without blame. She was by Mugabe's side, then a popular leader at home and abroad, during Gukurahundi. She was there as he centralized his constitutional power through the creation of the Executive Presidency. She was also said to have been involved in the 1988 Willowgate car importation scandal, one of the first national corruption scandals of the post-independence era.

Sympathy for her grew as she became increasingly ill with kidney failure in the late 1980s and Mugabe began his affair with a young married mother of one working as a typist in the president's office. In 1990, Grace Marufu bore their first child, Bona, when she was twenty-four years old and Mugabe was sixty-six. Early in 1992, Sally Mugabe died at the age of sixty. The president married Grace in a spectacular ceremony four years later.

Where Sally was loved for her apparent sense of modesty and public duty, Grace Mugabe became increasingly unpopular for her lavish lifestyle in the midst of the economic fallout of the 2000s. Aware of her imposter status, she began to style her expensive outfits in the mould of Mother Africa, buttressing this identity with highly publicized visits to orphanages and rural welfare projects.

In 2014, 'Amai Grace' began her foray into politics through her election as president of ZANU–PF's Women's League. As she ousted former Vice-President Joyce Mujuru from the post, she invoked old nationalist ideas of prostituting women to discredit the liberation war veteran, publicly shaming Mujuru with claims of video evidence of her as a 'mini-skirt wearer'. Invoking the raised fist often associated with Mugabe, 'Amai Grace' accepted her new role as head of the Women's League with a warning: 'I might have a small fist but when it comes to fighting, I will put stones inside to enlarge it, or even put on gloves to make it bigger. Do not doubt my capabilities.'

'Did you see her at the Bindura rally?'
'Ah, Mbuya, who didn't see it?'

'Heh, who knows what had gotten in that woman.'

Mbuya Chiganze starts laughing. I am visiting her in the New Year and we are watching the news on ZBC when President Mnangagwa's appearance triggers the memory of the infamous September 2017 rally for youth held in the town of Bindura in Mashonaland Central. It was there that 'Amai Grace' declared herself the incarnation of Mbuya Nehanda before denouncing the then Vice-President Mnangagwa and his wife as they sat next to President Mugabe behind her lectern. That the Mnangagwas had sat quietly through it all had shocked my grandmother so much that she called my aunt from her bedroom to come and see what this mad woman was saying. If she had been Mnangagwa's wife, Mbuya says, she would have told him, 'Baba, hembeyi.' Husband, let's go.

It was yet another performance of the public humiliation of senior political figures in Amai Grace's thinly veiled presidential campaign, as she consolidated power with the backing of her G40 faction, made up mostly of a younger generation of ZANU–PF members too young to have participated in the Second Chimurenga.

At her most bold, Amai Grace dared the veterans of the Second Chimurenga war to 'bring the guns', a stark contrast to Amai Sally who understood the politics of Chimurenga and her place in it as a woman. She had been in the trenches of the liberation war when Mugabe famously stated in 1976 that 'Our votes must go together with our guns. After all, any vote we shall have shall have been the product of the gun. The gun which produces the vote should remain its security officer – its guarantor. The people's votes and the people's guns are always inseparable twins.' Understanding this, Amai Sally led a post-independence rally of 'wives, widows and daughters of the revolution' in officially unveiling a monument commemorating those who had died, saying: 'We owe a lot to them. [This is] a symbol to us in the country to show that there were people who were really prepared even to die.'

In the last couple of years of his rule, as Mugabe increasingly faced challenges from his guns, the ultimate guarantors of his power, he took to contradicting his previous stance on leaders such as Tsvangirai being unfit to rule because they had no liberation history, declaring at a ZANU–PF Women's League meeting that 'politics shall always lead the gun and not the gun politics'.

By 2017, having acquired a doctorate in sociology with unprecedented speed for her thesis on changing family structures and children's homes in Zimbabwe, 'Dr Amai' became even more reckless and less inclined to Mother Africa pretences and took to wearing military-style berets atop bone-straight weaves. In a popular video clip that would find much airplay during the days of the coup, Dr Amai chose the pulpit of a massive interfaith rally at Rufaro Stadium on 5 November. It was here where she was allegedly confirmed by the divine as 'the chosen one'. Wearing a stylized version of the white cape of the conservative Apostolic Faith Church's women, she looked as if she was about to launch into a headbutt as she promised Mnangagwa, 'I will make you fall tomorrow,' before cackling gleefully with satisfaction. Indeed the next day, 6 November, President Mugabe fired Mnangagwa while he was out of the country, accusing him of plotting to take power through dubious means, including witchcraft.

A few days later, Dr Amai herself was made to fall, as part of the 'criminal elements' that the military was seeking to remove from the person of the president. Across the rallies and marches in Zimbabwe, many people re-appropriated for Dr Amai that tired characterization of troubling women, and sang, 'Hatidi kutongwa nehure'. We do not want to be ruled by a whore.

As ZANU–PF rebrands itself by sweeping all that went wrong into a Grace Mugabe-sized hole, this narrative of an errant step-mother is one often repeated in the homes of friends and relatives that I visit, 'Mudhara anga akaoma hake, asi mukadzi ndiye angaatadza, ndiye akanyanya.' The old man was stubborn, but the wife is the one who had done wrong, she was the one who was too much.

IX

President Emmerson Dambudzo Mnangagwa, his torso floating above in official portraiture on the arrivals wall of the recently renamed Robert Gabriel Mugabe International Airport, is the first to greet me as I return to Zimbabwe for the second time this year for Mbuya Chigumadzi's tombstone unveiling and memorial service being held the next day, 23 March 2018, in Murehwa.

As we take our baggage to the car, the conversation with family who have come to pick us up quickly turns, as has become the case, to whether 'things have changed' in 'Garwe's new dispensation'. My brother is one of those who say that they sense change as soon as they enter the airport. My parents too. I'm inclined to answer that it's confirmation bias. You will see what you want to see. The only thing that I see that has changed is the person in the official presidential portrait.

At a January rally, Mnangagwa, or 'ED' as he is known to most Zimbabweans, declares that in 'November, ZANU–PF, like a beast, went to the dip tank'. Indeed, 'Operation Restore Legacy' has brought about what feels like the end of petty oppression. We remain unharassed by police on the roads. In yet another masterstroke, after the de facto coup, which ironically ushered defence-force members such as the present Vice-President General Constantino Chiwenga into government, Zimbabwe is no longer *visibly* a military or police state. People take their new freedom to insult the person of the president as far as the pages of his actively managed social media accounts. The next day, Saturday 24 March, to our surprise, Murehwa, a traditional ZANU–PF stronghold, will see its first opposition rally in years as the late Morgan Tsvangirai's successor Nelson Chamisa holds court, incident-free. In April, I will attend a standing-room-only staging of a political satire, 'Operation Restore Regasi'.

Where, given the aim of 'restoring the legacy' of Zimbabwe's Chimurengas, you might have expected an African liberation stalwart to champion an Afrocentric development agenda rooted in the politics of land and resource sovereignty, Mnangagwa goes through the dip tank and emerges as Davos man. Wearing his now trademark Zimbabwe flag scarf, a relaxed and affable Mnangagwa declares to the world: 'Zimbabwe is open for business.'

It seems Zimbabwe is for sale. The indigenization policy seems to be all but scrapped as part of a national economic policy dependent on Foreign Direct Investment from the very same Bretton Woods institutions whose advice gave us the economic crash of the 90s. Of ZANU-PF's land policy, Mnangagwa has spoken of compensation for white farmers, declaring a break with 'outdated thinking'.

The new president also tries to clear what he can of his name on Gukurahundi, signing the National Peace and Reconciliation Commission Bill into law but remains under pressure to account formally and apologize for the post-independence genocide. In typical ZANU-PF fashion, he has refused individual responsibility, describing Gukurahundi as a 'moment of madness' resolved by the Unity Accord, saying: 'Overall we don't want to live in the past... From the past we must take the good that the past has in our history. And leave behind that which is bad. We don't want that to be repeated, ever, this is what I am saying.' The amount and variations of Gukurahundi denialism I continue to encounter with Shona-speaking friends, family, colleagues and acquaintances is upsetting, infuriating, crushing. If there is any real pressure for any meaningful accounting, it will come from the sites of the atrocities, Matabeleland, and to a lesser extent Midlands State, where people remain sceptical of Mnangagwa's overtures.

Whatever their pretences to the powers of persuasion in a genuine democracy, President Mnangagwa and his leadership are still interested in the pursuit of a divine right to rule over Zimbabwe. You don't, after all, take power in order to give away power.

On the very same day Mnangagwa declared that 'the people's voice is the voice of God', he flew to the shrine of Apostolic Faith prophet Madzibaba Wimbo, famous for his 1957 prophecy that Mugabe would rule Zimbabwe. During a 2015 visit by Mnangagwa, Wimbo prophesied that he would 'need assistance' to become Zimbabwe's leader. Not to be outdone, Vice-President Chiwenga made an appearance at the Noah Taguta shrine and in November 2016 Vice-President Mohadi made his way to the Enlightened Christian Gathering Church, where founder Shepherd Bushiri predicted that he would ascend to the second-highest office in the land.

Bushiri, who famously charged churchgoers R25,000 for a seat next to him at a 2017 dinner, is part of the proliferation of prophets and capitalist churches riding the last twenty years' swelling wave of 'fear industries'. In the face of economic hardship, many of our families have seen relatives die from curable and manageable illnesses, having been told by prophets to 'just believe', with believers then spending the last of their meagre earnings on 'airtime to heaven' and 'nights of salvation'. Spirit mediums have joined the profiteering too, the most successful being a Chinhoyi woman who, at the height of the 2007 fuel crisis, convinced a group of high-level government officials that she could produce refined diesel from rocks.

At a recent Zimbabwe National Gallery photo exhibition centring on the historic 18 November Solidarity March, my friend and brother (we share the same totem), the journalist Percy Zvomuya, reminds me of a conversation we had many years ago when I had first begun my research on Mbuya Nehanda. Former opposition leader and activist Sekai Holland had once told Zvomuya: 'VanaMugabe masvikiro avanaRhodes'. Mugabe and his people are the spirit mediums of Rhodes.

It is a bold statement to make. Cecil John Rhodes, the arch imperialist who did not feel it was enough to conquer this land and its people in his lifetime, sought in his afterlife to symbolize the spiritual conquest by ordering his burial at the spiritually sacred Matobos Hills, where our Ndebele, Shona and Kalanga ancestors and their spiritual leaders communicated with their god, Mwari.

It is a statement that has stuck with me all these years, until this moment. It strikes me that in a break from the spiritualism characterized by leaders such as Mbuya Nehanda, this highly individualized spiritualism invested in the delivery of miracles, divorced from the broader realities facing the collective, is itself a similar bastardization of the historic alliance between our spiritual and political leaders as they sought to fight collectively against the injustice of colonial rule for the benefit of past, present and future generations. Instead, we have leaders who, like Rhodes, seek to combine the power of the gun and the spirit in order to secure their individual right to rule.

Maybe it's because I'm both tired from the week's work and nervous about the grandchild's speech I'm supposed to give at tomorrow's memorial, but I don't make any flippant remarks about the new presidential portraits being the only thing to have changed.

On the drive 80 km due east from Harare to Murehwa, what my parents do say has changed dramatically since they left Zimbabwe in the early 90s, and even in the last few years, is the way people drive. It's a change they interpret as the frustration, anger and impatience of people who no longer care about much, let alone the rules of the road, as motorists continue to make a go at their own early deaths and ours too, making dangerous cuts at dangerous speeds even after nightfall.

Before we arrive, my parents try to help me with the speech I haven't started, saying it's okay if I speak in English, but I insist I want to do it all in Shona. They ask me what I want to say so they can help with the translation. I have many thoughts, but it feels a little difficult to say aloud, even if I have spent the last four months working on this book.

When we arrive at Mbuya's musha, the house my father grew up in, the first to greet me is Sekuru Justine, who came from Mutare a week ago as part of his familial duty to supervise the erection of his late sister's tombstone. 'Wakadii, Muzaya?' I tell him I am very happy to see him and we have a long conversation about the rainfall that eventually did come later in the year, before going to see the rest of the Chigumadzi, Dzumbira and Chiganze family members who had already arrived for tomorrow's service. We have supper here at Mbuya's old house and then we make our way down the road to the house my parents built in my great-grandfather's yard.

Around 5 a.m. the next morning, I draft the English version of my speech and then go to the room in our house that we knew as 'Mbuya's bedroom', because it was built as her wing and it was where she would sleep whenever she came to visit Murehwa from Harare where she had lived with my aunt, Tete Evie. Her absence is now filled by the presence of Mainini Foro, Mbuya Chiganze and another relative, Mbuya MaiPatience. Together, they help me with my translation. Mbuya Chiganze is a brutal editor, reminding me in her characteristically sharp tongue, 'Usanyanye kurebesa nyaya yako'. 'Don't make your speech too long.' I know Mbuya Chiganze finds my first conscious memory of Mbuya Chigumadzi difficult, the time the two of them had come to visit us in Durban, the last time we would see Mbuya walking, but she helps me as I try to find the best way to express the child's sense that nothing about her grandmother had changed even while the adults around her, she later learns, were in distress.

When my time comes, I still have tears from Tete Evie's daughter's speech and my mother's daughter-in-law's speech. With glasses to hide what I'm sure are red eyes, I begin. People are impressed and appreciate my deep Shona. They also appreciate its delivery in an accent which my father sometimes jokingly describes as 'rechiBlantyre', the accent of Zimbabweans of Malawian descent. Laughing too, I scold them without breaking my Shona, 'Teererai, munzwe. You people, you, instead of laughing, listen to what I am saying so that you hear my message. My Mbuya never used to laugh at my Shona, so you shouldn't either.'

I remain in Zimbabwe for several weeks after Mbuya Chigumadzi's memorial service and tombstone unveiling. In Harare, I stay with Mainini Foro in her 'Avenues' flat. It is a few streets away from Josiah Tongogara Avenue, the drive leading past State House which, had it not been for the military's intervention fearing a possible 'Gaddafi situation' on their hands, citizens would have stormed and, had he been there, surely taken Mugabe's head on 14 November 2017.

Josiah Tongogara Avenue is also the former site of the Msasa tree on which Mbuya Nehanda was said to have been hung on 27 April 1988. On 7 December 2011, witnesses said Nehanda's diseased and rotten tree was hit by a municipal workers' truck and collapsed onto one of its strong branches. The tree had stood unprotected in a central island. Despite it being seen as a traffic hazard, city authorities had resisted calls for the tree to be removed. The fall of Nehanda's tree coincided with President Robert Mugabe's national tree planting and reforestation campaign in Bulawayo as well as the annual ZANU–PF congress, its last major gathering before the 2012 elections. Nehanda's tree fell as the sacrilegious tomb containing Cecil John Rhodes remained a protected national heritage site. As her tree fell some of those municipal workers fled, believing it to be an omen of 'bad things to come'.

The Monday immediately following the memorial service for my grandmother, Mainini Foro and I drive the kilometre or so from the city centre to accompany Mbuya Chiganze to buy zvindarira, copper wristbands, to help with her sister's leg pains at Mbare's Mupedzanhamo – quite literally, the market where you go to finish your troubles, named originally for large imported second-hand clothing bales sold at exceedingly cheap prices. We go to the section you can find by asking for 'kweN'anga', where the healers are, or 'ma table anambuya na sekuru', for the stalls manned by the women and men selling traditional medicines, ritual implements and cloths from different regions in Zimbabwe and beyond. This, or Mbare market, was where I had been instructed to go to buy the powdered tobacco as gifts for Mbuya Nehanda's former spiritual aides in Dande.

The relatively young mbuya who serves Mbuya Chiganze and Mainini Foro is knowledgeable, and seeing my grandmother's age makes an unsolicited prescription for a powdered natural medicine from Matabeleland used for several ailments afflicting older women, a suggestion which is taken up.

'Mbuya!' This mbuya doesn't have the size of copper bands my grandmother is looking for, so she is calling out for another mbuya who calls another mbuya who ultimately does have the correct bands. The mbuyas work together like that.

While they wait for this market women's network to deliver Mbuya's ndariras, I walk around a little. In a corner of the market, I discover striking side-by-side murals of Mugabe and his former colleague, the late ZAPU leader Joshua Nkomo. Both of their youthful faces, Mugabe on the left, Nkomo on the right, are rendered in a beautiful grey hue. Black, yellow and green lettering declares Mugabe the 'CONQUERING LION of AFRICA', '... Shumba yemabhunu... (simbi ye basa)'. The great fear of the whites... (powerful leader), and below it 'SENT TO FREE AFRIKA'. Since I watched a video of a citizen tearing up Mugabe's face outside ZANU–PF's headquarters on the day of the 18 November Solidarity March, I have not seen any portraiture of the man who has become reduced to the figure of petulant grandfather. Beyond 'FATHER OF THE NATION', I do not catch the text accompanying Nkomo's portrait. A man sitting nearby becomes suspicious of my motives and begins questioning me, so I think it best to return to Mbuya and Mainini and their market women's network before I can take a photo.

I wonder what it is he is afraid of. Isn't this, after all, a new Zimbabwe?

X

Before I return to Zimbabwe for the first time in late 2017, my cousin, her friend and I form part of a small audience gathered at Johannesburg's Market Theatre for a one-night-only concert on 8 December by 'Zimbabwe's Mbira Queen' Ambuya Stella Chiweshe. We are mostly Zimbabweans; many of us here are seeking answers to questions about our two-week-old new Zimbabwe.

A few days later, Chiweshe becomes the first person I interview as I begin work on this book. I arrive early, and as I revise my notes, I begin to feel a deep, drowning sense of being overwhelmed. Part of it is that she reminds me of both my grandmothers. In particular, her tall frame and deep, reedy voice with which she sometimes flings out barbs, remind me of Mbuya Chiganze. I try to restrain myself from this familiarity. In a part of the world where black women have been forced into the often thankless and burdensome work of mothering both black and white children, I am always wary of making mothers of black women who have not chosen that role in my life. I try to stop the impulse, but the tears remain for the conversation I wish I had had with Mbuya Chigumadzi before she died just over two months ago, and for fear of the conversation I am determined to have with Mbuya Chiganze. My cousin reassures me by text, 'Nditete vako, ka,' reminding me that Ambuya Stella Chiweshe and I are both Shava of the eland totem, and so she is in fact my tete, a great-aunt in my founding ancestor's family. Over the next four hours, this great-aunt relays to me her own knowledge of the spirit of Mbuya Nehanda. Chiweshe is, she tells me, a granddaughter of Kaguvi's First Chimurenga spirit medium, and she relishes the opportunity to correct the misinformation her young and curious relation has picked up in her many books. This was to be my first lesson in the humility required for the many journeys in search of unanswered questions on which I was about to embark.

On the night of her concert, tall and regal in her long white kaftan, dreadlocked and barefoot, Ambuya Stella Chiweshe performs new songs and old hits for the intimate occasion which becomes a full-on celebration as she plays the most popular song of her career, 'Chave Chimurenga'. It's Now Chimurenga. In between sets, Ambuya tells us, her audience, that the music of the mbira dzevadzimu, the music through which we commune with the ancestors, is like water. We are after all, Ambuya says, made up mostly of water. And indeed, as you listen to the mbira it is like water washing over and through you.

Over a month later, the night of my visit to Sakubva in search of Mbuya Lilian's lost photo with Sekuru Justine, I am in a kitchen belonging to the family of late mbira player, Ephat Mujuru, in the village of Nedewedzo, at least 150 km north-west of Mutare. A bira is being held to thank the ancestors for the New Year; it is somewhere between night and sunrise, voices are singing and bodies are dancing in rhythm with the mbira and hosho in an endless cycle, creating the mouth through which those of the past can commune with those in the present about the future to come. I have the sensation of being bodyless, of being suspended in water, of being suspended in time. The waters of the ancestors, the waves of history, wash around me to combine the past, present and the future, flowing around me unending, absorbing some things and washing others away.

If Zimbabwean politics is a game of time and space and its manipulations, different powers find the moments most suitable to their agendas, freeze them, and insist on them to the exclusion of all other time. History, in our political game, is no longer a series of recurring waves carrying us all within them as our ancestors intended, but a straightforward line of progress for the few.

With Zimbabwe experiencing as much political turbulence as it has in just a generation or two, we find ourselves swept up by waves of massive historical transformations that ripple across time and space. For black women in particular, to consider the vastness of the waves of knowledge of our mothers, their words, their dreams, their songs, that have been lost to us through the innocuous fallibility of memory and the tongue, the violence of the colonial and the post-colonial almost seems unimaginable and impossible to grasp. The temptation then to concede these histories to those who are more powerful than us and have the ability to define us through it, becomes too great. And yet, if we still ourselves in the tumult to feel and consider the ways in which these historical waves have moved through our bodies and those who have gone before, we will discover that much has survived, passed down from breast to mouth, mouth to ear, ear to heart. Sometimes the vastness of what has been lost and distorted to us is there to be found by the most personal elements of history.

At a time where the official portraiture of the nation's new Father, Emmerson Mnangagwa, has been installed so that we may look up at him in our offices, hospitals, schools, airports, post-offices and stores, the act of imagining the lost portrait of Mbuya Lilian Chigumadzi has provided me with stable ground on which to reimagine her, to reimagine myself, to reimagine others, to reimagine the nation.

After years of staring up at the looming portrait of Mugabe waiting for our lives to change 'when the old man goes', a moment we came to think could only be occasioned by death, the moment has come and gone and we find ourselves where we were when we first began the wait. The wait for his departure weighed down so heavily on our hearts and minds that it constrained the spirit of radical political imagination that has allowed us to make and remake ourselves time and again over the centuries. In the same ways we limited our political imagination to the end of colonialism, with dire consequences for our post-independence years, Mugabe's end represented the end of our political imagination. Now that we are living through Mugabe's end, we will come to understand that Zimbabwe's future is not a matter of the old dying and the new being born.

To reimagine Mbuya Lilian's lost portrait is to begin to conjure up the gallery of portraits of African women erased from history through forced land removals, migrant labour, rape by baas and fellow comrades, the exclusion from post-independence land ownership, domestic violence, the treacherous roads of cross-border trading, HIV/Aids.

To imagine these portraits of women erased from the annals of official history is to confront our compulsion to erase and mitigate their image in the story of our making.

To reimagine the portraits of women such as Mbuya Nehanda who have been enlarged and frozen is to confront our compulsion to reframe and distort their image in the story of our making.

To imagine these women both named and unnamed is to face the historical present of both the physiological and psychological manifestation of cumulative, and inter-generational traumas and triumphs that have brought our nation here.

To imagine these women is to face their questions. They are difficult. They are painful. They are necessary. We cannot turn away even as we know in our hearts that we collectively fear facing these women because they will demand that their questions be answered. We know that their questions will release a torrent of granite boulders that will destroy the versions of us and the nation that we hold dear even as they harm us in ways untold. The force of their questions will surely crush the old certainties cast in Zimbabwe's great house of stone. And then, what will become of us? Who will we be?

If we allow ourselves the humility and courage to face up to these difficult questions, we will learn that this new way of being is not so new, it is of the present, past and future. This new way of being that we will create through our alternative histories will be created through a radical re-imagining of ourselves and the state. We are fearful and yet we know how to craft these stories, because, as the practice of our oral traditions tells us, history lives in the mouth, and so we must draw on memory and myth to craft these alternative pasts, presents and futures.

In this historical moment created with the backing of Zimbabwe's guns, it is important to face the unanswered questions of our mothers, grandmothers, sisters, aunts, friends and neighbours and indeed ourselves. To face these Big and Little Women is to confront the ways in which violence has been central to our self- and state-making. It is to face up to and consider the significance of violence in a context where the combination of the spirit and the gun was the only way we could overthrow our colonial adversaries. It is to acknowledge that we, falsely, continue to take for granted the historic alliance between our spirituality and violence.

A person is a person through others. This truth extends across time and space. We are through those who have come before us, those who have come with us and those who will come after us. Spirit possession, at the heart of Chimurenga, is an exercise in timelessness. It is those in the present communing with those in the past about the future concerning those who will come. Chimurenga has always been the intergenerational spirit of African self-liberation. It is not linear, it is bones that go into the earth and rise again and again.

BIBLIOGRAPHY

Principal Interviews

Basvi, Evelyn. Murehwa, December 2017.

Chiganze, Beneta. Makoni District, December 2017.

Chibatamoto née Mujuru, Monica – The medium of ancestor Sekuru Nehumba. Makoni District, 13 January 2018.

Chigumadzi, Freda. Zimbabwe, December 2017.

Chigumadzi, Peter. Zimbabwe, December 2017.

Chikara, Mai. Muzarabani District, 17 January 2018.

Chiweshe, Stella. Johannesburg, South Africa, 11 December 2017.

Dzumbira, Jane. Mutare, 26 December 2017.

Dzumbira, Justine. Mutare, 12 January 2018.

Gashu, Never. Karoi, 9 February 2018.

Kayerenga, Zvisineyi. Muzarabani District, 17 January 2018.

Manhenda née Mujuru, Stella – The medium of ancestor Sekuru Nehumba. Makoni District, 13 January 2018.

Mugwagwa née Manjengwa, Patricia – The medium of ancestor Sekuru Mushawatu. Makoni District, 13 January 2018.

Mujuru, Komboni. Makoni District, 13 January 2018.

Mujuru, Peter. Makoni District, 13 January 2018.

Mujuru, Zhanje. Makoni District, 13 January 2018.

Murenga, Mukomawasha. Johannesburg, 7 January 2018.

Books and Journal Articles

Amadiume, I. 1987. *Male Daughters, Female Husbands.* London: Zed Press

Auret, D. 1982. 'The Mhondoro Spirits of Supra-tribal Significance in the Culture of the Shona.' *African Studies* 41 (2): pp. 173–87

Barnes, T. 1992. 'Ideologies and the Construction of Class Amongst African Women in Colonial Zimbabwe, 1930–1960'. African Studies Institute Seminar Paper, University of the Witwatersrand, Johannesburg, 30 March

Barnes, T. 1992. 'The Fight for Control of African Women's Mobility in Colonial Zimbabwe, 1900-1939.' *Signs,* 17 (3): pp. 586–608

Beach, D. 1994. *The Shona and Their Neighbors.* Oxford: Blackwell

Beach, D. 1998. 'An Innocent Woman, Unjustly Accused? Charwe, Medium of the Nehanda Mhondoro Spirit, and the 1896–97 Central Shona Rising in Zimbabwe'. *History in Africa* 25: pp. 27–54

Bhabha, HK (ed). 1990. *Nation and Narration*. London: Routledge

Bryce, J. 2002b. 'Interview with Yvonne Vera'. pp.217–226 in Muponde, R and Maodzwa-Taruvinga, M (ed). *Signs and Taboos: Perspectives on the Poetic Fiction of Yvonne Vera*. Harare: Weaver Press

Bull-Christiansen, L. 1994. 'Tales of the Nation: Feminist Nationalism or Patriotic History? Defining National History and Identity in Zimbabwe.' *Uppsala*: Nordic Africa Institute

Chadya, J.M. 2003. 'Mother Politics: Anti-Colonial Nationalism and the Woman Question in Africa.' *Journal of Women's History* 15 (3): pp.153–57

Charumbira, R. 2008. 'Nehanda and Gender Victimhood in the Central Mashonaland 1896–97 Rebellions: Revisiting the Evidence.' *History in Africa* 35 (2): pp.103–131

Charumbira, R. 2015. *Imagining a Nation: History and Memory in Making Zimbabwe*. Charlottesville: University of Virginia Press

Chennels, A. 2005. 'Self-Representation and National Memory: White Autobiographies in Zimbabwe.' In *Versions of Zimbabwe: New Approaches to Literature and Culture*, edited by R. Muponde and R. Primorac (eds). 131–46. Harare: Weaver Press

Chigwedere, A.S. 1980. *From Mutapa to Rhodes*. London: Basingstoke and Salisbury: Macmillan

Chikowero, M. 2015. *African Music, Power and Being in Colonial Zimbabwe*. Bloomington: Indiana University Press

Chiwome, E.M. 1996. *A Social History of the Shona Novel*. Eiffel Flats: Juta

Clarke, M.F., and Nyathi, P. 2010. *Lozikeyi Dlodlo: Queen of the Ndebele*. Bulawayo: Amagugu Publishers

Coundouriotis, E. 2014. *The People's Right to the Novel: War Fiction in the Postcolony*. New York: Fordham University Press

Dladla, Ndumiso. 2017. 'Towards an African Critical Philosophy of Race: Ubuntu as a Philo-praxis of Liberation': Unpublished paper

Garlake, P. S. 1983. 'Prehistory and Ideology in Zimbabwe', in Peel and Ranger (ed), 1983, *Past and Present in Zimbabwe*. Manchester: Manchester University Press

Hanlon, Joseph. 2017. 'Land reform is a Zimbabwe success story – it will be the basis for economic recovery under Mnangagwa'. The Conversation. 29 November 2017. Web: https://theconversation.com/land-reform-is-a-zimbabwe-success-story-it-will-be-the-basis-for-economic-recovery-under-mnangagwa-88205

Hartman, S. 1997. *Scenes of Subjection: Terror, Slavery, and Self-Making in Nineteenth-Century America*. Oxford: Oxford University Press

Hegel, F. [1837] 1956. *Philosophy of History.* Trans. J. Sibree. New York: Dover

hooks, b. 1992. *Black Looks: Race and Representation.* New York: South End Press

Hunter, E. 1998. 'Shaping the Truth of the Struggle': An Interview with Yvonne Vera.' *Current Writing* 10 (1) pp.75–86

Jenje-Makwenda, J. 2004. *Zimbabwe's Township Music.* Harare: Self-published

Jenje-Makwenda, J. 2013. *Women Musicians of Zimbabwe: A Celebration of Women's Struggle for Voice and Artistic Expression.* Harare: Self-published

Kaarsholm, P. 1989. 'Quiet after the Storm: Continuity and Change in the Cultural and Political Development of Zimbabwe.' *African Languages and Cultures* 2 (2): pp.175–202

Kaarsholm, P. 2004. 'Coming to Terms with Violence: Literature and the Development of a Public Sphere in Zimbabwe' in Primorac, R. and Muponde, R. (eds). 2004, *Versions of Zimbabwe.* Harare: Weaver Press

Lan, D. 1985. *Guns and Rain: Guerrillas and Spirit Mediums .* North America: University of California Press

Lyons, T. 2004. *Guns and Guerrilla Girls: Women in the Zimbabwean National Liberation Struggle.* Trenton: Africa World Press

Martin, D. and Johnson, P. 1981. *The Struggle for Zimbabwe: The Chimurenga War.* London: Faber

Masuka, D. 1956. 'Nolishwa.' in M.J. Daymond, D. Driver, S.Meintjes, L. Molema, C. Musengezi, M. Orford and N. Rasebotsa (eds). 2003. *Women Writing Africa: The Southern Region.* New York: Feminist Press; Johannesburg: Wits UP, 2003. 245–46

Mkwesha, F. 2016. 'Zimbabwean Women Writers from 1950 to the Present: Re-creating Gender Images.' Dissertation presented for the degree of Doctor of Philosophy in the Faculty of Arts and Social Sciences at Stellenbosch University March 2016

Mlambo, A.S. and Raftapoulos, B. (eds) 2009. *Becoming Zimbabwe: A History from the Pre-colonial Period to 2008.* Harare: Weaver Press

Muchemwa, K. 2005. 'Some Thoughts on History, Memory and Writing in Zimbabwe.' In *Versions of Zimbabwe: New Approaches to Literature and Culture,* edited by R. Muponde and R. Primorac, 195–202. Harare: Weaver Press

Muchemwa, K. and Muponde, R. (eds) 2007. *Manning the Nation: Father Figures in Zimbabwean Literature and Society.* Johannesburg: Jacana Media

Mudenge, S. I. G. 1988. *A Political History of the Munhumutapa State, c. 1400–1902*. Harare: Zimbabwe Publishing House

Mudiwa, R. 2017. 'On Grace Mugabe: Coups, phalluses, and what is being defended' . *Africa is a Country*. 28 November 2017. Date accessed 31 March 2018:.https://africasacountry.com/2017/11/on-grace-mugabe-coups-phalluses-and-what-is-being-defended/

Mukiwa, FR. 2006. 'Women and Utterance in Contexts of Violence: Nehanda, Without A Name and The Stone Virgins by Yvonne Vera'. A dissertation submitted in partial fulfilment of the requirement of Degree of Master of Arts in English in The School of Literary Studies, Media and Creative Arts, Faculty of Humanities, Development and Social Science, University of Kwa-Zulu Natal, 2006

Muponde, R. and Maodzwa-Taruvinga, M. (eds) 2002. 'Introduction' pp.xi-xiii in Muponde, Robert and Maodzwa-Taruvinga, Mandivavarira (eds) *Signs and Taboos: Perspectives on the Poetic Fiction of Yvonne Vera*. Harare: Weaver Press

Mupotsa, Danai S. 2014. 'The Oppositional Gaze,' in 'White Weddings', Unpublished PhD thesis, University of the Witwatersrand

Mutondi, P. B. 2012. *Zimbabwe's Fast Track Land Reform*. London: Zed Books

Mutswairo, S. 1956. *Feso*. Oxford: Oxford University Press

Mutswairo, S. 1988. *Mweya wa Nehanda*. Harare: College Press

Ndlovu-Gatsheni, S.J. 2009. *The Ndebele Nation: Reflections on Hegemony, Memory and Historiography*. Rozenberg: UNISA Press Series

Ndlovu-Gatsheni, S.J. 2009. Do 'Zimbabweans' exist? : *Trajectories of Nationalism, National Identity Formation and Crisis in a Postcolonial State*. Bern: Peter Lang

Nkomo, J. 1984. *The Story of My Life*. London: Methuen

Oguibe, O. 2004. *The Culture Game*. Minneapolis: University of Minnesota Press

Oyèwùmí, O. 1997. *The Invention of Women: Making an African Sense of Western Gender Discourses*. Minneapolis: University of Minnesota Press

Pazvakavambwa, S and Hungwe, V. 2009. 'Land Redistribution in Zimbabwe' in Bingswanger, H, Bourguignon, C and Brink, R. *Agricultural Land Redistribution. Towards Greater Consensus*. The World Bank, Washington DC, 2009

Raftopoulos, B. and Yoshikuni, T. (eds). 1999. *Sites of Struggle, Essays on Zimbabwe's Urban History*. Harare: Weaver Press

Ranger, T. 1967. *Revolt in Southern Rhodesia 1896–7: A Study in African Resistance*. London: Heinemann

Ranger, T. 1970. *The African Voice in Southern Rhodesia, 1898–1930.* Evanston, IL: Northwestern University Press

Ranger, T. 1982. 'The Death of Chaminuka: Spirit Mediums, Nationalism, and the Guerrilla War in Zimbabwe.' *African Affairs* 81, no. 324: pp. 349–69.

Ranger, T. 2002. 'History Has its Ceiling. The Pressures of the Past in *The Stone Virgins.*' In Muponde, R. and Maodzwa-Taruvinga, M. (eds). *Signs and Taboos: Perspectives on the Poetic Fiction of Yvonne Vera.* Harare: Weaver Press

Ranger, T. 2004. 'Nationalist Historiography, Patriotic History and the History of the Nation: The Struggle Over the Past in Zimbabwe.' In *Journal of Southern African Studies.* 30 (2): pp.215 – 234

Samupindi, C. 1992. *Death Throes: The Trial of Mbuya Nehanda.* Harare: Baobab Books

Shamuyarira, N. 1965. *Crisis in Zimbabwe.* London: Andre Deutsch

Sithole, N. 1968. *African Nationalism.* Oxford: Oxford University Press

Sithole, N. 1977. *Roots of a Revolution: Scenes From Zimbabwe's Struggle.* Oxford: Oxford University Press

Smuts, JC. 1930. *Africa and Some World Problems.* Oxford: Oxford University Press

Staunton, I. (ed). 1990. *Mothers of the Revolution: The War Experiences of Thirty Zimbabwean Women.* Harare: Baobab Books

Sylvester, C. 2003. 'Remembering and Forgetting 'Zimbabwe': Towards a Third Transition', in Gready (ed). *Political Transition, Politics and Cultures.* London: Pluto Press

Trouillot, M-R. 2015. [1995] *Silencing the Past: Power and the Production of History.* Boston: Beacon Press

Vambe, L. 1972. *All Ill-Fated People: Zimbabwe before and after Rhodes.* London: Heinemann

Vambe, M.T. 2002. 'Spirit Possession and the Paradox of Post-colonial Resistance.' pp.127-141 in Muponde, R. and Maodzwa-Taruvinga, M. (ed). *Signs and Taboos: Perspectives on the Poetic Fiction of Yvonne Vera.* Harare: Weaver Press

Vambe, M.T. 2012. "Aya Mahobo': Migrant Labour and the Cultural Semiotics of Harare (Mbare) African Township, 1930-70' in F. Demissie (ed). *Colonial Architecture and Urbanism' in Africa Intertwined and Contested Histories* Farnham: Ashgate Publishing

Vera, Y. 1993. *Nehanda.* Harare: Baobab Books

Vera, Y. (ed). 1999. *Opening Spaces: An Anthology of Contemporary African Women's Writing.* Johannesburg: Heinemann

Walker, A. 1983. *In Search of Our Mothers' Gardens : Womanist Prose*. London: The Women's Press

Willis, Deborah and Carla Williams. 2002. *The Black Female Body: A Photographic History*. Philadelphia: Temple University Press

Wilson-Tagoe, N. 2002. 'History, Gender and the Problem of Representation in the Novels of Yvonne Vera.' pp.155-178 in Muponde, R and Maodzwa-Taruvinga, M (ed). *Signs and Taboos: Perspectives on the Poetic Fiction of Yvonne Vera*. Harare: Weaver Press, 2002

Yoshikuni, T. 2007. *African Urban Experiences in Colonial Zimbabwe : A Social History of Harare Before 1925*. Harare: Weaver Press

Zvomuya, P. 2016. 'The Resilient Mugabe'. *The Jacobin*. 26 August 2016. Date accessed: 31 August 2016. <https://www.jacobinmag.com/2016/08/robert-mugabe-evan-mawarire-this-flag-zimbabwe/>

ACKNOWLEDGEMENTS

Mbuya

There have been many people who have brought me to this point. In particular, my extended family on the Chigumadzi, Chiganze and Dzumbira sides who have made this a collaborative project in ways I didn't expect.

Mama, Deddy, Farai.

Mbuya Beneta Chiganze. Sekuru Douglas 'Teacher' Chiganze. Sekuru Kenneth Chigumadzi.

Sizwe Thandukwazi Nxumalo.

Tete Ellah Wakatama Allfrey.

Emma Paterson.

Sekuru Justine Dzumbira. Mbuya Jane Dzumbira.

Tete Evie Basvi. Mukoma Lilian Chigumadzi.

Mainini Foro Chiganze.

Sekuru 'Uncle Charlie' Chiganze. Sekuru Ben Chiganze.

Sekuru Timothy Chiganze. Mbuya Barbara Chiganze.
Mbuya Rumbidzai Chiganze.

Thato Magano. Percy Zvomuya. Thando Mgqolozana.
Danai Mupotsa. Bongani Madondo. Sisonke Msimang.
Ayabulela Mhlalo. Antoinette Tidjani-Alou. Tariro
Muzenda. Nqobizita Ndlovu. Tanya Charles. Bongani
Ncube. Thamsanqa Netha. Zibusiso Ncube. Munya
Furamera. Amanda Furamera. Rangoato Hlasane.
Sisipho Moorosi. Nqobizita Ndlovu. Bhekisizwe Peterson.
Sharlene Teo.

Mbuya, these are some of the people who have made it
possible for me to complete this tribute to you. If the
book has failed at any turn, it is all me.

Muzaya Pana
HARARE, APRIL 2018

INDIGO

Sign up for our newsletter and receive exclusive updates including extracts, podcasts, event notifications, competitions and more

www.theindigopress.com/newsletter

Follow The Indigo Press

@PressIndigoThe
@TheIndigoPress
@TheIndigoPress

Subscribe to the Mood Indigo podcast

www.theindigopress.com/podcast